How To Save Your Marriage In 3 Simple Steps

Lee H. Baucom, Ph.D.

ISBN-13: 978-1492902430
ISBN-10: 1492902438

DEDICATION

For my ever-patient and supportive wife, Kathy.
And for my wonderful children, Maggie and Harrison.
You have taught me to be a husband and father.
You have all my love!

CONTENTS

INTRODUCTION

Every book has a story. This book is no different. The story of this book starts in my childhood. I was fortunate. My parents were (and are) happily married, giving me a great model of togetherness. Their marriage also provided a shelter from the world, a safe place to be.

But that model did not extend elsewhere. In my extended family, I witnessed a number of divorces, several both painful and destructive to the families involved. And I watched as my friends had parents divorce. While I was at a safe distance, I did see the pain and hardship that resulted. And for the life of me, many times, I could not explain (or get an explanation of) what happened. It seemed a mystery.

In college, I was exposed to Family Systems Theory. This theory helped me to understand the individual as a part of the family — and the family as a system of interconnected people with multiple dynamics. This led me to pursue post-graduate work that focused on marriage and family.

At the same time I started my graduate work, I was blessed to marry my wife, Kathy. That was one great decision on my part! Kathy has supported my dreams and aspirations, even when they have been a bit far-fetched. And I hope we have supported each other, building a marriage that will last for our lifetimes. Perhaps there, more than anywhere else, I have learned about myself, relationships, and love. There is nothing like on-the-job training!

After graduate school, I started my career as a therapist. But some of my disillusionment with the whole therapy model was already present during my graduate school days. I constantly pushed on the limits of the theory. And my concerns were often verified in studies and in experience.

So I started trying to piece together what worked and what made sense. That led to, in 2001, my writing a little ebook, Save The Marriage. That ebook has grown and grown into the larger Save The Marriage System. Quickly, I found my days filled with working on the website, the material, and with the clients that followed. I soon found that marriage issues had become my central focus.

But in 2002, I fell ill. Not just a little bit sick, but life-changing sick. For weeks, I struggled through feeling bad, stubbornly refusing to go to the doctor. When I finally did go to the doctor, he was puzzled. It took two more visits before my doctor realized what I had. My diagnosis was Sarcoidosis. Generally, this is a chronic, long-term illness that disables and eventually kills. I was quickly cast into the medical system, seeing a number of doctors in a number of specialties.

What I remember most was the call my wife took from my doctor. It was after-hours and he used his first name. Those are not good signs! He told my wife that he thought there was an 85% chance of my being permanently disabled. The only fact I could process was that my healthy days may well be behind me. . . and I hadn't even known to enjoy them!

As sick as I was, I was fortunate.

It turned out that I had the acute version of the illness. Even before I was in to see the specialist (after a three month wait), I was beginning to recover. It was a long six months of struggling back to health, trudging through each day in pain and discomfort. But I did recover. I still feel the odd effect of the illness here and there, reminders of those frightening days. But I can now look back upon that as a turning point.

From there, on, I realized I was living on "bonus time." I had another chance. And I also knew I had more to do in the world. Part of that "more to do" is to help where I can, to provide guidance where possible, and to show paths toward healing and wholeness. Interestingly, my overall passion has always been about thriving — and that came into sharp focus after losing my health and then regaining it.

What you have in your hand is part of my wish to provide more ways of thriving. I do not intend on just providing a guide on how to stop a divorce or stop a crisis. My belief is that you can build a marriage that is thriving, not just surviving. I realize that we may have to start from a tough spot, but your marriage can turn around. Your marriage can find traction, even in the midst of a crisis, and grow toward something wonderful.

I invite you to join me on this journey. Let's agree to walk through the tough spots together, waiting to see the amazing marriage you create on the other side! Remember, out of pain and discomfort comes growth and strength. I just ask that you hang in there and work through. There IS a better place for you and your marriage.

Let's get started!

CHAPTER 1
WHERE WE ARE HEADED?

You may have heard the quote, "Life is a journey, not a destination." The same is true for a marriage. It is a journey that can have many mountains and valleys, curves you did not see coming, and challenges you never anticipated. But it is still a journey. The destination always remains down the road, calling you to keep moving.

This book is designed to help you on that journey. It is not a book about the journey at the top of the mountain, where you can both enjoy the vista and see your direction. This book is about the valleys; where you don't know what to do and are not sure if the journey will even continue.

My job is not so much to be your tour guide as to be your survival and rescue expert. While I would love to tell you about ways to enrich your relationship, that will have to wait for another day. Right now, we want to be looking at first-aid — what to do so that your marriage does not deteriorate further. So this is more a survival guide.

But here is the interesting thing: if you learn the survival tactics, they are the same methods and ideas that will allow you to create a thriving marriage down the road. The same toughness and assuredness that one gains from facing adversity will be the same flexibility and ability you will bring into your marriage as it improves.

Many people ask me, "Why does marriage have to be so difficult?" First, trust me when I tell you that it does not have to be difficult. But the task of marriage is not about avoiding difficulties. It is about knowing how to survive them when they come.

Marriage is THE most intimate relationship a human can have (or at least it should be). When there is that level of closeness, both in proximity and emotions, there are going to be issues and frictions.

A marriage crisis is less the result of the difficulties and more the result of the inability to solve and heal the difficulties. As these points of friction and conflict pile up, the foundation erodes until the underpinnings of the relationship begin to falter.

To use the metaphor of a journey, imagine taking a wrong turn. But instead of stopping and rectifying the situation, you continue to make another wrong turn on top of another. Soon, you are lost. You may be a quarter of a mile off the highway, but you can't see it and don't know how to get back there.

Often, a couple decides to stop trying, even thought they may be one turn from getting back on-track. Instead of finding a way back (or stopping to ask directions), the couple just decides to give up on the journey. Instead of learning some navigation skills, they either continue to wander aimlessly or just sit down and quit the journey.

How about you? Where are you in that process? Has one or the other of you simply given up, ready to stop trying to find your way back? Have you both decided to perhaps take a pause and learn some skills to get back onto the trail? Or perhaps you have realized, after just a wrong turn or two, that you are off-track and need to stop and get back on-track before things get worse?

I have good news: there are navigation skills and survival skills that you can learn and master. And with those skills, you can get your marriage back onto the right path. You can help get your marriage back onto the journey, headed in the direction that will keep you fulfilled and happy in your relationship for the rest of your lives.

The Survival Mindset

Before we get started, let's work on building your survival mindset. This is an important precursor as we move into those important skills. How you think about your marriage survival will certainly impact how well you implement the skills we will discuss in the coming pages.

I have a strong interest in what makes people resilient, and more than that, what helps people to thrive. As part of that interest, I follow the survival literature. This is not the literature of "survivalists," those that plan for disaster. Instead, it is the study of how people actually respond in the face of crisis — how do people survive real accidents and disasters.

Research shows one very common theme: there are clear skills of survival (for example, if you are lost in the woods, how to stay warm, dry, hydrated, and likely to be found). But the single-most important factor in who survives and who does not has to do with mindset — how people mentally approach their situation.

Mindset is not just about survival situations, but about how we go through life: Is life difficult or a challenge? Are you stuck where you are or can you grow and adapt? Is it "not your fault" or is it your responsibility? (We will discuss these issues in detail in the following pages.)

So what is it I mean by mindset? Mindset is how you approach your situation and events in your life. It is how you cope, adapt, and respond to difficulties. Your mindset is your overall attitude and approach to dealing with the ups and downs of life.

This is not the same as optimism. You may not be optimistic, but you may still have a strong survival mindset. And here is the really important point: a mindset can be assumed. It takes no special skills. Only a willingness to believe that something more is possible.

You may tell me that you have always had a survival mindset, a belief that you could make it through any difficulties. "Great," I would tell you, "It will serve you well here."

But you may tell me that you have either never had that mindset or never needed it before. This highlights an important issue: a survival mindset is built out of needing it. If you have never had a challenge or needed this mindset, you would not have cultivated it. But now that you are faced with a difficulty, it is time to adapt and build that mindset.

Begin with simply telling yourself this: "I CAN learn to deal with these difficulties. I CAN learn the skills I need in order to get through this. I CAN work through these challenges and come out stronger."

Challenging The Can'ts

Did you notice all of those "CAN's" above? They are there for a reason. Over and over, I hear people say "I can't. . . ." They place a limit on what they can and cannot do, and there are many times in which the "can't" is self-created and does not exist in real life.

In fact, "CAN'T" comes in Four different flavors. One is false, two can be fixed, and one (rarely) is true. While we say "I can't" on a regular basis, it is only partly true and only in the minority of situations. So let's take a look at the three areas.

Four Types of Can'ts:

1) You can't do something because it is not possible.

This type of "can't" is really about physical impossibility or some other genuine limitation. This is not the same as "It is not likely." For example, I can't make myself invisible (just to push the extreme), as it is physically impossible (at least as we understand science right now). But if I say "I can't meet the President," that is just an unlikely. Perhaps I know someone, several connections removed from me, that does know the President, and with enough effort, I could meet him.

Let's take an example from relationships: I can't go back in time and take back something I did or said. Again, within the limits of science right now, it is not possible to do this. It is, however, possible to learn from that incident and grow. It is possible to make amends and work to have a different relationship while being a different person.

2) You can't do something because it hasn't happened yet.

This is really a matter of tenacity and persistence. Sometimes, we say "I can't ________." That is really an indication that it just hasn't worked yet. I was talking with a friend that was just starting to run, after letting himself get out of shape. He told me, "I can't even run a mile." While that was currently correct, if he continued to work at it, he would then be able to run a mile, plus more! So I said, "How far can you run?" He told me, and I suggested he just keep working to increase it. Two weeks later, he told me he was running a mile.

Let's take an example that may be more apropos. I often hear, "I can't connect with my spouse." Often, this is a statement that it has yet to happen. It is not impossible to connect with a spouse, but it might take effort in a particularly disconnected marriage. So effort becomes important. Sticking with it becomes important. Then, "I can't" moves to "I can, just not yet."

3) You can't do something because you don't know how.

The second type of "can't" is based in a lack of knowledge. I can't do brain surgery (and have the patient survive!) because I do not have the knowledge and skill base for that task. But the task, itself, is not impossible. It is more a lack of my knowledge or skill-set.

In relationships, you may say "I can't connect with my spouse," but see that it is actually possible to do so. You just don't have the knowledge or skills to do it. The nice thing about this "can't" is it is changeable. You CAN gain the skills or knowledge you need to change it.

My friend, the neurosurgeon, did not have the skills or knowledge to do brain surgery until he went to med school and trained. The difference was only in his acquisition of the knowledge and skills.

In this type of "can't," it can feel daunting. You may realize that you don't know how to do something, but can at least see that it is possible. You may see that gaining those skills may cause discomfort — both in effort and in changing yourself, but you can see that it is possible.

In this area, you can say "I can't. . . yet," and recognize there is a way to change the "yet." At that point, it becomes "I can."

4) You can't do something because you won't.

This is a crucial distinction. Because when we get right down to it, MANY of our "can'ts" are really "won'ts." Enough that changing this one factor in your life can transform you. But the first step is realizing when this is the case — when you are saying "I can't," but what you really mean is "I won't." "I won't" is a choice. But it is not a choice until you make the shift from "can't" to "won't."

When you make the shift in understanding, you may realize that you can make that shift to "I will."

Let's look at a few common ones:

• "I can't forgive my spouse (or myself)." vs. "I won't forgive my spouse (or myself)."

• Forgiveness is always a choice to make, and mostly so that YOU can move forward. (We will cover more on this later.)

• "I can't connect with my spouse." vs. "I won't connect with my spouse."

There are many ways to connect with your spouse. Perhaps you have tried some approaches that have not worked, and have given up. But there are other options. Have you truly exhausted the options? (We will cover more on this later.)

• "I can't change who I am and how I act." vs. "I won't change who I am and how I act."

We all can change and grow — or we can refuse to change and grow. Life is ALL about growth and development, so when we tell ourselves about how we can't change, we have only imposed our own limitations. (We will cover more on this later.)

To be very clear, I do not want to infer that every "can't" is false. I only want to point out that often, when we say "can't," there are some steps we might take to turn it to a "can." Let me suggest a couple of steps to determine the difference.

Discovering The Difference Between Can't and Won't

You can quickly assess the difference between "can't" and "won't," as long as you are willing to be candid and honest with yourself. In fact, it will painless and easy. You will want to simply ask yourself two questions:

1) Ask "Why not?"

Challenge yourself. Why "can't" you do something? Really think through the reasons. It is simple to give a pat and quick "I can't. . . " and not consider the reality.

Remember, much of our "can'ts" are really about our current mindset (something we will cover later), and mindsets are limitations we self-impose. The only way around them? Challenge them! Find a more useful mindset.

2) Ask "How can I?"

This question will begin a creative thought process. "I can't" limits you. "How can I?" opens up the possibilities. You will only answer this question by being creative and open to possibility.

Not only that, but if you begin answering "How can I?" with possibilities of action or attitude, you disprove the "can't." You show that the "can't" really isn't a "can't." Then, it is a matter of deciding upon whether it is something you don't know how to do (a matter of acquiring knowledge and skill) or it is a "won't" (which then gives you the option of changing that to "can and will.")

A Survival Mindset Is NOT Just About Surviving But Thriving

The first step to upgrading your survival mindset is to get rid of those unnecessary "can'ts." The next step is to view yourself as a person of possibility and potential.

Some research shows that our minds bombard each of us with somewhere around 65,000 thoughts each day. The same research shows that 95% are the same as the day before. More importantly, approximately 80% of the thoughts are negative or pessimistic in nature.

An important part of a positive approach to life is not to challenge all of those negative thoughts, but to realize that they are happening. When they exist in the background, we don't even notice them, but our psyche pays the price. Once we are aware of them, we can recognize one very important fact: **they are just thoughts.** There is nothing magical or true about a thought, just because it is a thought.

Minds are designed to create thoughts, some great and some not so great. The danger is when we forget this fact and begin to believe everything our mind tells us. Sometimes, it is just a mechanism of the mind making thoughts.

Instead, we can begin to look for the thoughts that leave us thriving. Remember, thoughts are just thoughts. They are not real and do not necessarily even represent any truth. So choose to focus on the positive and useful and only notice that the negative ones can keep you stuck.

You can make a realistic assessment of a situation, but then choose to focus on the possibilities and opportunities. For example, "Our marriage is in crisis and we are disconnected." That is a good assessment. Following that up with "And there is nothing I can do to change it. I am a horrible person that somehow deserves this," does nothing to move you forward. It only keeps you immobilized and self-critical. Another thought, "So what can I do to change this and move us toward connection?" opens up tremendous potential of change and creativity.

Adopt a thriving mindset and you will have created a survivor's mindset. You will know that you CAN make it through this and every other difficulty.

What's Coming Up

It is now time to turn our attention to addressing the problems and issues in your marriage. I promised to show you how to save your marriage in 3 simple steps. In the next pages, I will show you exactly how to do this. But let me be clear: "simple" is not the same as "easy."

When I tell you there are 3 simple steps, I promise you that is the case. I do not promise you that the steps will be "easy" or "effortless." I will only promise they will be fruitful and fulfilling. Are you ready to take on the challenge?

In the coming few pages, I want to talk a bit about some ways to cause more problems in your marriage — not so that you can make things better, but so you know some traps to avoid.

After that, I want to give you some understanding on what went wrong, how you got to this point in the relationship, and how you can begin to make some changes.

From there, you will be ready to take on the 3 Simple Steps. I will help you understand each of those steps and give you some specifics on how to move through these steps.

Let me show you the path, so you don't have to wander around. Your map follows. Will you join me for the journey?

CHAPTER 2
HOW **NOT** TO SAVE YOUR MARRIAGE!

You are no doubt reading this information because your marriage is in trouble. In fact, other than therapists, I have never seen a person read a book on how to save your marriage who was NOT in the midst of a real marriage crisis. (We therapists often read books about painful issues. Such reading is good for helping clients, but not so good for our own mental well-being and cocktail party talk!)

Before we talk about what to do to save your marriage, I think it is also important to cover what things many people actually do when there is a marriage crisis — things that are actually counter-productive. There are some very clear things you want to be doing, but there are also many things to avoid.

Here is my Top 10 Ways to NOT Save Your Marriage! This is only a partial list of the mistakes I see people make when they want to save their marriage. Sometimes, it is best to learn from others' mistakes, rather than make them yourself.

Let me tell you now: if you see some things on this list that you HAVE been doing, don't worry. None are show-enders. They may create more resistance on the part of your spouse, but none are insurmountable. But if you see things you are doing on this list, it's time to stop! If you haven't done any on this list, keep avoiding them! It will make your progress faster.

Top 10 Ways to NOT Save Your Marriage!

10) Do nothing! Don't worry, the crisis (problem, situation, incident, threat, etc.) will pass!

This is the old "bury your head in the sand approach!" The reality is, it is very unlikely that the crisis will simply pass. Let's be honest: over time, this strategy builds up more and more resentment, then finally, everything falls apart. You can act surprised at that point, but you will know, deep down inside, that you ignored things way too long.

It is a cumulative effect, a marriage crisis. Rarely is there one "precipitating event" that suddenly ends the marriage. Instead, it is the problem ignored that adds to all the other problems ignored, which finally creates so much frustration that the "house of cards" falls.

So, the first useless strategy: just do nothing!

9) Refuse to get any outside help. Who needs it? You can do this yourself!

When you are in the middle of a marriage crisis, it is not time to "figure it out!" One of my favorite quotes is from Albert Einstein, "The same level of thinking that created the problem will not solve the problem." In other words, when we only use the thought processes and mindsets that led us into trouble, we will not find a way out of the problem.

We all get stuck in our thought patterns. Once we establish them, we don't change much. Think about it: don't all of your spousal arguments basically follow the same pattern. Doesn't your daily routine pretty much go the same? We like "sameness," and change is a bit of a threat. Even the painful sameness is better than the unknown — at least that's what we tend to believe.

The problem is that we find ourselves stuck, without outside help and information, nothing will change, even if you want it to. "Outside help" can include lots of things: therapists, coaches, ministers, groups, retreats. . . and you happen to have one in your hands right now! Be sure the source is sound, then make sure you take advantage of outside help.

8) Grab some "free advice!" Hey, free is good, right?

Almost always, free advice is worth about that — nothing! When you are injured, do you seek out some "free advice" on that injury? Or when you need some legal advice, do you just get some "free advice"?

So why, when your most important relationship is on the line, would you just try to use some free advice? Look, we live in a "transaction society." We make trades and transactions to get what we don't have. And knowledge is no different. People who give away advice are rarely giving away anything worthwhile.

The real question is this: if free is your goal, how much do you REALLY treasure your relationship? If I told you how to save $20,000 instantly, would you pay for it? Well, that is the minimal cash value of your failed marriage. In other words, a divorce in the U.S. averages $20K. Save your marriage, save $20K.

And what about having a wonderful, loving, peaceful marriage? What is the worth of that? Really, what price would you put on that? I ask because I know plenty of people who think nothing of grabbing a $4 coffee drink every day, a couple of $3 packs of cigarettes every day, a $30 bottle of wine on the weekend, subscribe to a $150 cable service, blah, blah, blah. Then, when they go looking for advice to save their marriage, they want to find some free advice.

It is always about value — and the value you place on your marriage. Free advice? It is probably more costly than you can ever realize in the long run.

7) Get some good books, and then leave them on the bookstand. Maybe your spouse will at least think you are doing something!

We authors don't like to admit this, but statistics show that upwards of 80% of self-help books that are bought are never read. Imagine that! The answer may be right there! You took the time to get a resource, either because the cover looked nice, somebody recommended it, or because you were desperate.

Then, onto the bedside stand it goes, underneath the magazines, the daily paper, that good novel. . . then suddenly, it is lost.

The very bit of information that could save your marriage is stuck at the bottom of a stack, never to be read. Sound familiar? If so, it's time to dust off the information and give it a read! At least give it a chance. You've already invested your money in it. Why not give it a test drive?

6) Read the information, but then don't do anything! It won't work in your situation, anyway!

OK, so you dusted off that information, and even read it. . . but then you took no action! Maybe the information seemed impossible, far-fetched, too easy, too complicated, or just dead wrong! Now you do need to use your better judgment, but perhaps it is worth a try!

What you've been doing has clearly not gotten the results you wanted. So, perhaps it is time to try something new. Sometimes, new thinking seems foreign, unnatural. But it is really like anything new: repetition builds skill. What seems awkward begins to feel more natural. Suddenly, what seemed impossible seems elementary.

Again, remember Einstein's quote about thinking. It also applies to action. Doing what you've done hasn't gotten you what you want. What's the risk of trying something different?

5) Get bad information from unqualified sources. Hey, any information is better than no information. . . right?

As you have likely already discovered, there are lots of "experts" willing to make a buck to tell you how to save your marriage. Be sure your "expert" is really just that. At a minimum, make sure they actually have some training, not just their own experience (especially of a failed relationship)! They don't have to have a Ph.D., but if they can't tell you about their training, other than "been there, done that" about their own marriage, move on!

Experts are experts because they have worked in the field, received training, and have some ideas on how to help you. The others are experts in marketing. Be sure to distinguish between the two.

Remember way back when the barbers who cut hair were also the "doctors?" They weren't trained and caused lots of damage, but that was the only choice. Well, we don't live in the "Wild West" anymore, and there are plenty of real experts. Get their advice and avoid the damage of well-meaning but ill-equipped "experts."

4) Do everything at once! Hey, if a little is good, a lot is better. . . right?

Wrong! Many marriages have suffered from neglect for too long, until one day someone wakes up and says "enough." Then the other person jumps into high gear! They try to make "date nights," meaningful conversations, do the housework, get another job, buy expensive gifts, plan huge trips — just about anything to make it work!

Instead, pick a couple of things. Be consistent with them and try a slow approach. Building from zero takes some time. But if you try the "everything at once" approach, you will scare your spouse away.

3) Argue, beg, plead, and show your emotions. Surely your spouse will see your sincerity to save the marriage!

This is a very common situation. You see, we all are master "scriptwriters," often ready for Hollywood. . . at least in our own minds! We assume a spouse will see the wisdom of our logic, emotions, begging, and pleading. The problem is that they are working off a different script — the one they are writing (and certainly not yours).

People are natural resisters. Our minds just naturally pull against whatever we see as opposition. If I throw someone a rope and when they grab it, I start pulling, their reflex is to pull back, matching power with power. It is no different in verbal tug-of-war. The harder I try to convince someone of something counter to what they have said, the stronger the reflex for that person to become even more entrenched in the belief.

There is a technical term here: Psychological Reactance. This term refers to the fact that we naturally rebel against an opinion when it feels forced upon us. And we will rebel against it, even if we agree with it! When you argue, beg, and plead, your spouse will feel you are forcing your opinion and naturally resist — even if your spouse actually agrees with you. Creating more resistance is not a good strategy.

So the arguing, "reasoning," begging, and pleading have the opposite effect and actually hasten the dissolution of the relationship.

2) Let your spouse know your theory about how this is really about your spouse's "issue." Then your spouse will see how unhealthy he/she is!

Here is how to throw even more gas on the fire: when your

spouse says he or she wants to leave, point out how:

a) It is about their midlife crisis,

b) They are never satisfied,

c) It is really about their dysfunctional family,

d) It is about some other diagnosis you read about or saw on Oprah or Dr. Phil.

You may be dead-on! The problem is that you are not going to be seen as an objective provider of a diagnosis. Instead, you will only be strengthening the sense of frustration that your spouse is feeling. Diagnosis is best done, if at all, by an impartial and outside expert or by one's own self.

Resist diagnosing your spouse. It will backfire.

1) Try to prove how much you need your spouse! Surely, just seeing he or she is needed will get your spouse to stay!

Neediness is never attractive and when someone wants to leave, feeling the neediness only throws fuel on the fire. People want to be wanted, but not desperately needed! And in the midst of a crisis, the last thing someone wants is to feel manipulated.

I have seen people threaten to kill themselves to prove how much they need the other person. I have seen people refuse to pay bills, eat, take care of the kids, take care of the house, etc., etc., etc. And in every case, the person who wants out says "See? This is why I need to leave." It's hard to argue with that. Being needy is never attractive and it is even more unattractive when someone wants nothing more than to not be needed.

Do not set out to prove how much you need your spouse. You may want to begin helping your spouse understand how much you want your spouse in your life — but that is very different than need. Desire/want is attractive, while need is repulsive in a relationship.

Well, that is MY top ten list of how NOT to save a marriage while trying to save it. I could go on for many more; I think I have seen every mistake possible. However, I know how creative people can be. So this list is a starting point to help you avoid some pitfalls that I have seen.

My hope is not that you become discouraged, but that you think through what you are doing and how you are doing it as you try to save your marriage. There is no more noble or heroic task in today's society than trying to hold a relationship together. I just want to stress the need to do so in helpful, not harmful ways.

Which brings us to the topic of how to stay on-track in your efforts. Because there is one more "Don't:" Don't be inconsistent (more on this later). Find your direction and stay on track.

CHAPTER 3
STAYING ON TRACK

We are here, you and I, for the very same reason. We are here to save your marriage. I am here to be your virtual coach, providing the information and encouragement you need. You are here to get a new perspective, gain some new tools, find some new understandings of your situation, and TAKE ACTION.

In this process, we are partnering together. Let's make some agreements together. First, I promise that I will be giving you the best information I can. After a quarter of a century of working with couples, I know what works and what doesn't. I have a clear understanding of why marriages get into trouble, and more importantly, I know how marriages get out of trouble. I realize this is a frightening and confusing time for you, so I want to take that information and boil it down to the essentials for you.

Next, I ask that you promise to take action and do what you can to save your marriage. Remember, "doing what you can" is different than "doing whatever." One is about taking measured, accurate, planned action. The other is about throwing everything at it.

The first option, "doing what you can," is about having a plan and sticking with it. The other, "doing whatever," is about following every idea you have or have read, regardless of how it fits into your approach.

Let's look at this from a different angle. And let me assure you that this example comes straight from my life. Let's assume that life has thrown you a little "wakeup call," and you realize you need to take action to get into better health and shape. So, you decide to change your eating and start exercising. You start looking around and find one place that says "eat less fat," and another that says "eat complex carbs," and another that says "eat no meat," and another that says "eat no carbs," etc., etc. There are LOTS of ideas, and several are likely to work. . . but only if you consistently follow the plan. Otherwise, you make no progress. If you do everything, you will either be eating everything or be eating nothing.

Then, you decide to exercise, so you start looking for some information. One says "do cardio," and another says "do strength training," and another tells you to "do interval training," and then one says "cardio is dangerous," and another says "strength training won't help," and another suggests using machines, but another suggests using weights. Pretty quickly, the process becomes overwhelming, and you may end up doing nothing. . . unless you do some research to pick the best approach, and then do it!

You can always fine-tune any plan as you move forward. But doing this plan, then this plan, then this plan — all giving you conflicting advice, will do little to move you forward. Choosing an approach that you have researched and that makes sense, then sticking with it, that is what improves your life (in any area).

So I want you to approach this in a similar manner. In the next little bit, let's cover some basic information, talk about the 3 Simple Steps involved in saving a marriage, create an approach, make a plan, and then stick with it.

In my efforts to take better care of myself, I have noticed a few important details. First, there is a glut of information around us. You can always do more research and look for better approaches. I am not opposed to more information. I AM opposed to letting the "get more information" approach keep you from either 1) doing nothing, or 2) doing everything. It is possible to get stuck looking for the "perfect" answer, which is really just an excuse for doing nothing. It is also possible to do a little of this, and a little of that — then wondering why you don't see results.

Notice that either approach ends up being a lack of commitment to action and results. When someone is ready for a change, then the next step is to find a solution (notice that it doesn't have to be "the" solution), followed by the next step of acting on the solution.

Which brings us to your actions.

Let's be very clear: what I will tell you is very simple. A reminder: do not confuse simple with "easy." My approach is not complicated and full of psychological jargon. My approach is represented by research and practical testing, "in the trenches," as they say. But that is not the same as "easy to do." I will challenge you to think differently and act differently. And change takes effort.

More than that, marriages do not get into trouble overnight, with a single event. There may be events that point to the fact that the marriage is in peril, but they are only highlighting weaknesses already there. One event may be the touchstone that demonstrates the problems, but that does not mean the problems have not been developing for weeks, months, and usually, years.

There are many "last straws" in relationships, but to stay with that analogy, there were lots of "straws" that came before. The "straw that broke the camel's back" is yet another point, another symptom, of the underlying problems.

So it may take a bit of time to gain traction. It may take continual effort, built over a period of time, to begin to see a shift. If you were the captain of a cruise ship and decided to make a turn in direction, it would take some time and distance to begin to see the shift. You are moving a huge ship that has momentum and is moving through an ocean of water, and any action will only show over a period of time.

It is no different with your marriage. The two of you have gained momentum, even if it is in a less-than-healthy direction. It will take some time to shift the momentum and start moving in a healthy direction. Don't be discouraged!

Seeing few immediate results does not mean anything. In fact, that is more the exception than the rule. Some marriages, in the early stages of a crisis, see very immediate results. But the deeper and longer the crisis, the longer it takes to see a shift.

Let's make a commitment now, you and I, that we will continue working on this, even if there is no immediate shift. Commit to yourself that working on the relationship is worthwhile and that you are going to "stay the course," once you have made your course correction!

Remember the reasons why you are working on the marriage, why you have committed to saving the marriage. Some may say it is easier to walk away, so here is some support to explain why you are making the effort.

Some Reasons To Stay On Track

Commitment. Marriage is based on a commitment, a promise. That promise is one with no "outs," really. When you promise you will be with someone "for better or worse, in rich days and poor, in sickness and health," there are not many "days" left. And that commitment is what creates the powerful bonding that is only possible in marriage.

When you make a promise, in front of friends and family, it is a commitment. A commitment is something you say, to remind yourself of what you want to do, during the moments when you no longer feel the way you did when you made that commitment. So, you rely on the commitment that you made.

Commitments will pull you through the tough spot and get you to a better spot. Commitments are what we stick with when the days are tough. The reward for doing so is a fulfilling, loving relationship.

Love. Sometimes, people forget this one, because they confuse it with the warm, gushy feeling of being "in love." But love is much more than that. It is about connection and bonding with someone. And we tend to underestimate the pain that breaking that bond creates. In other words, most people underestimate the pain that will come when a divorce happens.

Children. For some time, a number of books proclaimed that children are not (or at least "need not be") harmed in a divorce. But consistent research shows this is not the case. While it does not mean that children will always suffer lifelong wounds, it is clear that divorce has a strong effect on children. The one relationship they see as permanent and stable is destroyed. It often causes a child to wonder about all loving relationships. More than that, most children assume that some part of the marriage problem is their fault — in spite of what parents say or do.

Just one more reason to stay together is "for the kids." It is not reason enough to stay in a miserable marriage, but reason enough to transform the miserable marriage into a great marriage.

Finances. Practically speaking, divorce is financially devastating. The cost of the average divorce in the United States has been estimated at upwards of $20,000. That is the direct cost, including legal fees and losses on divided property. And that is the cost, not the overall financial effect. This is the value that disappears from the joint assets, not including the fact that each person has likely lost half of the financial resources before that $20,000 or more is removed.

Happiness. Most research shows that, in spite of wishful thinking, people are NOT happier after a divorce. In fact, the level of life satisfaction actually declines for the vast majority of people who divorce.

People tend to overestimate relief that will come from the divorce and underestimate the emotional impact that will come from the divorce. When we are in pain, we often want to just escape. But the pain of marital discord is better healed than escaped.

Again, these are not reasons to stay in an unhappy marriage. They are reasons to transform your marriage from an unhappy marriage to the marriage you would treasure and of which you would be proud.

Your Options

In your marriage and in just about every area of life that is unsatisfying, there really are three options:

1) You can continue on the same path you are on. You may know the pain of the current path. But you may decide to simply continue down this same path. Many people do this by default. On a daily basis, they just continue to move in the same direction, even if it is painful and unsatisfying.

For some people, this is a calculated decision, based on other factors: getting children through school, waiting for economics to improve, not having an option of somewhere else. But for most, this is just a daily lack of decision — continuing to move in a painful direction by default.

2) You can abandon the situation. For a marriage, this means getting a divorce. It is the option of just giving up on the current situation and jumping into a new situation. In cases of abusive relationships, this can be exactly what needs to happen. (NOTE: I am NOT in favor of working to save an abusive marriage. Personal safety is too important in such situations.) But for most marriages, this is not a necessary move.

3) You can transform the situation. This is where you see the possibility of something being different than what it has been. It is about creating a marriage that you treasure. This is the path of the information in this book. Sometimes, you need some help to see the new possibility. Sometimes, you need some tools in order to transform the situation. That is what we want to address in the coming pages.

Ready to transform your marriage? Let's get a few more building blocks in place, then let's get started!

CHAPTER 4
WHY MARRIAGES GET INTO TROUBLE

The Trajectory of a Marriage In Trouble

"Paul" and "Sherry" were seven years into their marriage. They had been together for ten years. But now, two children and a mortgage into the marriage, they were not sure if they could go on.

Both Paul and Sherry noted how much love each felt for the other during their dating days, and into the early days of their marriage. In fact, neither can really point to any one event that was a turning point. It seemed to be more an accumulation of events and moments, mostly unnoticed by each of them.

Over time, each turned attention to other areas of life. Both focused on their children, throwing themselves into child activities — usually each going in a separate direction. Sherry built a very tight community with her "girl-friends," meeting for lunch and play dates.

Paul found common interests with people at work. Several became interested in triathlons, and Paul joined in. Soon, he was involved in a.m. and p.m. workouts, disappearing for long periods of time. Several weekends each year, Paul competed in these intense athletic events.

At one of those events, Paul met a fellow competitor. They were able to talk about training strategies and exercise routines. Then they started chatting about their personal lives. Over time, their texting, phone calls, and emails grew to a point that Sherry took notice. She realized that Paul had replaced the connection they once shared with someone else. This other woman became a growing concern for Sherry. Paul seemed unaware of the danger. He just knew he was happy to have found a "soul mate."

"All happy families resemble one another, each unhappy family is unhappy in its own way."
Leo Tolstoy

In terms of marriage, I am going to have to disagree with Tolstoy. Unhappy marriages arrive at unhappiness in very similar ways. The details may vary just a bit, but the overall pattern is disconcertingly similar.

While marriages each have their unique problems, all marriages follow a pattern of connection, and many follow a similar pattern of disconnection. It is this pattern that is so predictable from situation to situation. Your relationship will likely be reflected in this very pattern of coming together and falling apart.

Let's look a bit at the process of both coming together and falling apart.

One important point to understand is that the process of dissolution of the relationship, if a marriage goes in that direction, is a mirror image of the process of connecting. In other words, in the same way you came together, you fall apart, unless you escape the downward trajectory.

Here is a map of that process. We will examine the details below.

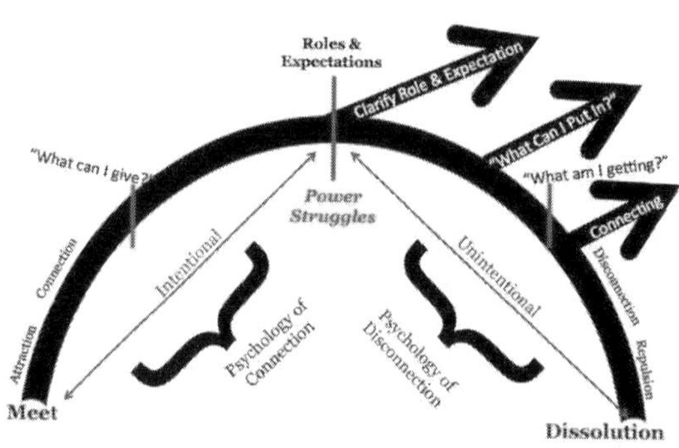

The Psychology of Connection

Let's look first at the building of a relationship, the Psychology of Connection. Any couple first meets as individuals. For whatever mysterious reasons, there is an initial attraction. Somehow, both have a mutual attraction to traits in the other. Perhaps it is appearance or outward personality. Perhaps it is interests or aspirations. Whatever the unconscious attraction, they "click."

From that point, each works to build the connection. Each asks the question, "What can I give to this relationship?" This creates a growing connection between the two that feeds off of the connections that each is working to establish. At this point, the relationship is self-nurturing and snowballs into "falling in love." The feeling of connection overflows to a feeling of love and passion. This process is intentional, meaning that both people are intentional about working to connect with the other.

At some point, every relationship, once connected, must find its rules and roles. Two people can only float around in the connecting phase for so long before there has to be some establishment of how the couple will get through life. What are the roles that each will play? What are the expectations that each has for the relationship and the other person? This inevitably leads to some level of **power struggle**, as each attempts to define him/herself, the other person, and the relationship.

There is a decision to be made at this point: "Do we come together as a team, or do we continue to struggle?"

If a couple can become a team, a *WE* (which I will describe in detail later), they can escape the other side of the process, the Psychology of Disconnection.

Many people ask when the power struggle starts. The answer varies from couple to couple. Sometimes, it is early on in the relationship (and continues for a long while for some couples). For other couples, it does not start until the early days of marriage. It is hard to avoid the struggle and negotiation, though, for very long into a marriage. It is very hard to be in such an intimate relationship without defining the expectations and roles. It just happens naturally. (Notice that "naturally" is a different word than "struggle-free." The process can be very difficult and full of struggle.)

The Psychology of Disconnection

On the downward side of the arc, we find the process of a relationship that does not escape the trajectory. This is the process of **disconnecting**.

In my work with premarital counseling of couples, I notice that without exception, people marry because they want to show their love for the other person. They want to spend their lives expressing this love and being in connection with the other person. Even with the strong element of wanting the other person in their lives, there is the outward movement of energy toward the other person.

Interestingly, when couples come to my office with a marriage in trouble, a shift has happened. Instead of looking for how they can love the other person, each person is looking for how their spouse is loving them. In other words, the energy has reversed. The prior focus of "How can I love you?" shifts to focusing on "How are you loving me?" This focus quickly shifts to "What am I getting out of this?"

One of the Relationship Coaches in my organization told me that his marriage was on the rocks and was transformed when he stopped asking "What am I getting?" and started asking "What can I give?" The shift allowed him to reconnect and reach out again toward his spouse.

There is a built-in scarcity mindset that comes from the perspective of "What am I getting?" That question gets us to focus on lack: lack of love, lack of attention, lack of energy, lack of care, etc., etc., etc. What we focus upon, we will find evidence to support — even if that "evidence" exists more in our mind than reality.

"What can I give?" is a question of potentiality. It assumes there is an endless amount of love and affection, which a couple can share together, when that is the focus.

You will notice that asking the question, "What can I give?" is the second exit point from the downward and unconscious trajectory toward dissolution. The question only comes when one or the other person makes a conscious choice to shift.

If the couple does not make that shift, the next level is a growing sense of **disconnection**. At this point, either or both can make a choice to reconnect, to nurture the connection between the two.

This conscious choice to reconnect moves the couple make to a sense of connection, of being a *WE*, and they can again escape the trajectory.

At each point of potential escape, the effort and energy required to escape the trajectory grows. "Gravity" takes over and accelerates the energy of the disconnection. Minor issues require minor readjustments. Major issues require major readjustments.

As the disconnection grows, so do the chances for separation, affairs, divorce, and abandonment. The need for connection, as we will discuss shortly, is so strong that there grows a sense of desperation to find that connection somewhere.

The human need for connection is similar to the human need for nourishment. If we don't get enough food, anything edible begins to be inviting. Junk food or snacks can quickly replace real meals. And desperate enough, humans will consume trash to avoid starvation. Starving for attention is no different. The need will be met, in healthy or unhealthy ways.

And as this process of disconnection continues, it leads to the opposite of attraction: **repulsion**. The person who once attracted the other becomes the object of repulsion. Instead of the "rose colored glasses" that many wear in the process of falling in love, there are "dark colored glasses." These glasses only show the negative elements of the other person, dimming the good and positive aspects. Just as we are selective in looking at the positive during the process of falling in love, we become selective in looking at the negative when the disconnection moves to repulsion.

As we move through this book, we will be examining the ways to rebuild the connection, in an attempt to restore the nourishment to the relationship. It is time to shift away from the "junk food connection" and move to "health food" that truly nurtures the marriage.

Self Growth or Self Stagnation?

"If you plan on being anything less than you are capable of being, you will probably be unhappy all the days of your life."
Abraham Maslow

Stuck. Stagnant. Is that where you are? That is where many people are. Some people are stuck everywhere in life. Others have areas of growth and areas of stagnation. How about you?

It is interesting to me that life seems to be designed around growth, and yet we humans seem to want to stop our growth. We get to a certain point in life and make a decision (conscious or unconscious) to stop developing and growing.

Perhaps it comes from the false notion that at some point, we should "arrive," be complete, and "all grown up." If that is the case, any growth or movement tends to be a sign of having not quite made it there.

Studies of professionals (doctors, attorneys, therapists, etc.) show that their professional libraries tend to show copyrights prior to the year they completed their training. In other words, for the most part, they studied the current literature — current for the period in which they trained — and then stopped.

Sure, there are continuing education events. But many professionals show little change in their theoretical and practical approach to their work. In other words, they stopped growing.

The same thing happens to all of us, in many areas. In relationships, we find "what works" with someone and we keep doing it. "Functional" and "effective" are different. You can find a functional approach to something, and yet it is not maximally effective. So even if an approach is not the best, we keep doing it, if it works.

Remember that trajectory of a relationship? It starts with a curiosity about another person and leads us on a quest to learn about them and to learn how to relate to them. But over time, if we are not careful and do not continue growing the relationship, the pattern devolves into a disconnection.

There is a similar trajectory for our personal lives. When we come into the world, we are naturally curious. There is not much that can hold us back. We explore and gradually we learn how to explore even better. We are sponges of information and action.

At some point, we decide we are "grown up." We stop being as curious. We stop wanting to grow. Growth, it seems, is sometimes seen as immaturity. But I love a quote from Ray Kroc, the founder of McDonald's, that points us in a different direction:

"You are either green and growing or ripe and rotting."

Kroc nails it. There is no arriving. You are either on an upward arc, or on a decline. There is no static position. Just like a relationship cannot be static (it is either growing or declining), a human cannot be static. We will either be growing or rotting, to paraphrase Kroc.

Just for a moment, I want you to do some self evaluation. How are you doing in several categories? Are you in a growth pattern or a stagnation pattern?

Mind

Are you engaged in learning about new things?

Do you continue to develop interests and hobbies?

Do you take in information that challenges you to continue to develop your psyche?

Do you challenge your mind with new ways of doing things?

Do you seek out views that are different than yours, not to change your own, but to consider other perspectives?

Do you nurture connections with other people?

Body

Do you seek better ways to care for your body?

Are you finding new ways to challenge your body?

Do you find ways to be active, regardless of your situation?

Soul/Spirit

Do you seek moments of engagement that are meaningful?

Do you seek a sense of purpose in your life?

Do you find activities that engage you at deeper levels?

Assess yourself on areas in which you may want to start learning again. Are there points in your life that you can continue growth or reengage in growth? What would that look like in your own life? What would that look like in your marriage?

For many people, there are areas in which they are still growing, and there are areas in which they are stagnant. I remember meeting with a couple that had grown disconnected. The man kept proclaiming, "You can't teach a dog new tricks. I just can't be expected to learn how to talk with my wife, or how to be romantic, or how to solve a conflict better. This is just who I am."

I asked him, "Do you say the same thing about work? Because I noticed that you were out at a sales seminar the other day, and you went to a time management seminar a couple of weeks ago. Why did you go there, if an old dog can't learn?"

This man was an active learner in several areas of his life, but had stopped applying that engagement to other areas of life. He truly believed that he was not capable of a change in those relationship areas — in spite of the fact that he was constantly learning better ways to work.

I have to give him credit. From that day, forward, he committed to learning how to be a better spouse and a better person. He realized he could learn and made a decision that he would grow.

What, you might ask, does this have to do with saving your marriage?

YOU Are The Greatest Tool You Have For Saving Your Marriage!

How you show up in your relationship and in life, who you believe yourself to be, how you interact with the world, and who you are becoming — these are the elements that you bring into your marriage.

If you have grown stagnant, I can guarantee that your relationship has grown stagnant. You bring yourself into the marriage. If you have grown stuck, your relationship will be stuck.

When you grow, you bring energy into your life. When you bring energy into your life, you also bring energy into your relationship. When you bring energy into your relationship, the relationship has new potential and possibility.

More than that, a stagnant person is not an attractive person. Few of us seek relationships with someone who is stale and stagnant. The vitality that people find attractive is not there. And part of your task in saving your marriage is having a spouse ***want*** to be in a relationship with you.

****Was there a little piece of your mind that just said, "Why should I have to work to attract my spouse?"** Well, let's be clear. A loss of attraction is part of the downward trajectory, as discussed in the previous section. The fact is, even in a good marriage, we all want to be attracted to our spouse. It is simply the nature of intimate relationships. And when that attraction is missing, you can work to be more attractive and you can work to see more that is attractive in your spouse. Don't let the "should's" — what "should" or "should not" be dominate your thoughts. Go with what you "can" do.

And even more than that, if you don't grow and develop, your perspective will not change. A change in thought and perspective is all that will bring a potential change into anything. A paradigm shift is needed. The same thought patterns that got you to the point of a crisis will keep you in that crisis.

"We cannot solve our problems with the same thinking we used when we created them."
Albert Einstein

We ALL have areas in our lives where we can grow and expand. We ALL have areas where we are stuck. We ALL have potential for raising our "personal standard."

Standards

A "standard" is what you expect of yourself, the standard of your own personal interactions with the world. Standards are almost always ready for an update. You can always raise what you expect of yourself. That takes you to a higher level of interaction with the world.

Notice that I did not say you can always raise your expectations you have of others. You CAN decide how you will be treated — what someone can or cannot do to you. That is a "boundary." You can set a boundary that stops another person's behavior toward you. But this is different than an expectation you might have of how they will act in the rest of life.

Let me clarify with an example: you may have a standard that you will be honest with everyone. You can expect that you will be honest and truthful (however you define this) with those with whom you interact. You cannot expect that others will always be honest. You can wish that, but you will likely be disappointed. You can set a boundary that if someone is dishonest with you, there will be a consequence (not a punishment, but a consequence) designed to keep someone from being dishonest with you.

You cannot affect what they do in the world, however. Let's say, for example, that you have children. It is beyond your control to make them be honest with everyone. You can decide that you will be honest, and you can have a boundary that there will be a consequence if someone is dishonest with you, but someone may be dishonest with everyone else.

I offer this clarification because I see many people who try to place a standard onto another person, be it a spouse, child, or friend. Usually, it only leads to frustration and struggle.

For the sake of clarity, let us define it one more time:

Standards: What you expect of yourself in how you will interact in the world and treat other people.

Boundaries: What you will NOT allow someone to do to you.

(For this guide, I will not be discussing boundaries, but you can find an entire section on boundaries in the Save The Marriage System.)

Sometimes, growth and development come from one simple action: raising your standard. Not just raising a standard, but committing to living out that standard. In other words, there is the standard that people claim ("I will be honest with everyone around me") and the standard they live ("Being dishonest in this situation is okay. It keeps me out of trouble, etc."). So both stepping into a standard and truly living it, then stepping up to that standard, is an excellent method of escaping stagnation.

Your Meaning and Purpose

When a person becomes stagnant, it is often a sign that the person has also lost connection with what makes life meaningful and purposeful.

When we lose track of our place of meaning and purpose, we tend to be lost and wandering. When there is a sense of meaning in what we do, and it feels that we have a purpose to follow, our internal compass automatically calibrates to this "North Star," and it pulls us through life. We have a place from which to make decisions. We have a direction toward which we can move.

We all need that sense of meaning and purpose in our life. And for just a moment, consider the people you find to be magnetic or attractive. Are they typically people who seem to have a sense of purpose? Are they people that navigate life by what is meaningful? The same is true for anyone who reconnects with a sense of meaning and purpose.

These two words are closely associated, so let me tell you what I see as the differences.

First, **meaning** is what we derive from what is happening to us and around us. Being with family or friends can be meaningful. Being in the midst of a spiritual experience, be it in the middle of the woods or the middle of a religious service, can be meaningful. Experiences, both good and bad, can be meaningful. Meaning is something we see within the moments in which we live.

Purpose, though, is something we pursue. It is a direction in which we head. There may be activities that give us that sense of purpose. There may be a goal or value that aligns with our activities that fills us with a sense of purpose. Purpose comes from moving toward an ideal or belief. For example, people may find a sense of purpose within a career. This is not limited to doctors or clergy. For example, a real estate agent may find a sense of purpose in helping people to find a home (and not just a house).

What is *your* place of meaning and purpose? It is something which you must define for yourself. And you will know it, because when you find it, you will find your energy elevates and your mind comes to life. Find your "soul glow," and you will know you are once again navigating by the North Star of meaning and purpose.

Working on your own sense of meaning and purpose WILL impact your marriage. When you are on your purpose and finding meaning, you are fundamentally a different person than when you are "coasting" or "floundering."

At this point, you may be wondering why these points about your personal development arise around the issue of saving a marriage. It is a crucial part of the process. In fact, it will become one of the steps you will follow in the coming pages.

As we move forward, you will discover that knowing the trajectory of a relationship and understanding your own stagnation will create the beginning points for how you will save your marriage. They are foundational understandings that will lead to the 3 simple steps that will save your marriage.

CHAPTER 5
THE **KNAC** PROTOCOL FOR CHANGE

People often ask me, "What are the elements of saving a marriage? What do I need to do in order to get started?" You see, saving a relationship is far different from almost anything else you're going to try to tackle in life. Because it is an entirely new arena, you are faced with an entirely new challenge.

Earlier this week, I received an email from a person who bought my Save The Marriage System two years ago. After using the System, he asked me for a refund because his wife left anyway. The reason he was writing me was to tell me that after we refunded him, he continued to use the information. He continued to try to reach out and connect. He continued to try to find some ways of bridging that gap between himself and his wife. His wife was involved with another man when they separated.

Over time, his efforts began to work. Sometimes, these things take time and energy and "stick-to-it-iveness." He kept trying, and then one day, she came back and said that the other relationship was not what she wanted. She wanted to rebuild their marital relationship. It took awhile for his efforts to sink in, but it worked.

We can't always be sure of where it's going to work, but we do know that efforts to save marriages do work. Some marriages cannot be saved, regardless of desire or effort by one person or even both people. But many can be saved, with the right approach and information. A primary difference between the two is the willingness of one person to act, to keep moving forward, even when it seems to be impossible.

I have an interest in health and well-being. I have always had an interest in well-being: why people do well, why people thrive in life, and why people are successful. But the health part, I must admit, I neglected for my own for years. . . until I got sick. When I got sick (we thought that this illness would be life-threatening if not life ending), I got a wake-up call from my body, from the universe and wherever else those things come. I got a wake-up call about how I had been neglecting my health. I'd been working on my mind, soul, and spirit, but not on my body. My body had gotten out of whack.

I was extremely sick for four months, and it took another six months to recover. I still feel twinges from that incident.

So I got interested in how to get into shape and how to eat better. Here's the interesting thing: you know that if you start exercising, then you will get in better shape. Now you can't guarantee that somebody can become a world-class athlete or that they are going to be a bodybuilder — Mr. or Ms. Olympus. But you can guarantee that if somebody takes better care of themselves, they can get into better shape.

That's not the same with repairing a marriage. Working on a relationship is different, with no guarantees.

When I was a child, I did a lot of magic. I performed a lot of magic shows and was a pretty decent magician. Many people thought I was a talented and entertaining magician and hired me for lots of shows. I realized that becoming good is a matter of practice. If I wanted to learn a trick, I just needed to practice until I could get it. It took effort, it took energy, it took interest, but I could master it.

Working on a relationship is little bit different than that. The difference is you have a spouse who may or may not cooperate with your attempts to save your marriage. I can't guarantee what a spouse will do. I can only guarantee that I know what sets the frame for people to save their marriage, if it's savable. There are people who use my material and still end up divorced. There are people who use my material — and it takes two or three years before they see the results. But, there are people who turn the relationship around quickly, because they do a few things right. And in my mind, it's an approach that has three things. These three things have to go together in order to have the framework, the groundwork, to save your marriage.

The KNAC Protocol for Change

These three things form my **KNAC Protocol for Change**: you have to have **Knowledge**, you have to take **Action**, and you have to have **Courage**. All three pieces have to all be in place in order for there to be a significant change in any place in your life.

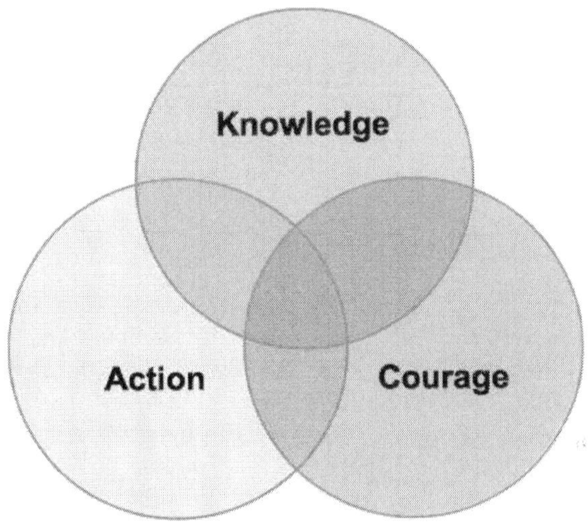

KN-owledge: There's so much information available these days. In any area, you've got to find something that makes sense to you. In saving your marriage, whether you use my System or other people's work, whatever makes sense to you, choose that information. You've got to have knowledge that shifts your thinking.

You don't have to know everything, and you don't need to be getting a PhD in marriage therapy. I did that, along with other experts, so you don't have to! But you need to be getting the knowledge that will get you started right. I've met plenty of people who have built a knowledge base for themselves: they have 35 books on improving their marriage; their Kindle is full of info on improving their marriage; and they have purchased several courses on the Internet and have DVDs. They have all this information, and they do nothing but consume it. Knowledge is a piece of the puzzle, but just a piece.

You have to know what you're going to do; you have to have a direction. What really gets couples into trouble is that they didn't have a knowledge-base to get there; they don't know how to get to a successful marriage. It's a very sad thing that we do such a poor job of training people to have a successful marriage. People don't know what they're getting into; they don't understand what marriage is truly about. I know that because I do the premarital counseling with couples, enough to know that they don't really understand the target. Nobody ever told them what the target is, and they didn't have parents who could show them.

Couples have little direction, few maps, and not much information to make the journey from the altar to the successful marriage. And the sad fact is that the path is quite simple. It is just misunderstood or unknown.

I have to say now, here's what you're trying to do: You are trying to build a *WE*, to stay connected, and to build teamwork. You are trying to create that place where you know that you can rely on each other — that you have each other's backs. And not just your backs, but your fronts, your sides and everything else. You need the understanding that you're going to get through life together, no matter what it throws at you.

If you get that, you've got it. You know the direction. From there, we just have to build in the information on how to become a WE, what to do when that understanding is missing or lacking, and how to actualize the relationship through the events of life.

So there's a knowledge base about the nature of marriage and how to regain a troubled relationship (we will cover this in the coming pages). Then there's an action base.

A-ction: Knowledge points toward action, but only when we make a shift away from the "why's" of knowledge. Sometimes, it is easy to get caught up in diagnostics. People have a deep desire to answer "why" something is the way it is. And that is as far as it goes. This is much like going to a doctor to find out what is wrong with you and then doing nothing to treat the issue the doctor discovers.

While few of us would ignore our medical conditions, many of us do ignore issues of personal development. The tendency is to get caught up in why something is the way it is and then do nothing to take action to change it. Instead of acting, many times, people simply decide "That's just the way it is. What can I do?" And they stop without answering the question of what they can do.

No change can happen unless there is action. No plan you create and no knowledge you digest will change anything until there is action.

But "just taking action" is not the solution. Because many times, the problem is people take action that is based in fear. We are easily pulled into that "fight/flight" mode of taking action by either struggling or fleeing. These are, indeed, actions. They are just not actions that will move you forward. Instead, they are reactive.

So, there is a need for another ingredient that shifts reaction to response.

C-ourage: Many people gain the knowledge and know the action to take, but then they let fear tell them not to do the necessary work. Fear is a normal part of life. It is ever-present. Courage is what makes the difference. Courage is not a lack of fear, but choosing to act in spite of fear. It's choosing to set fear aside and say "You know what? I'm going to try this anyway." People often say, "I think I want to save my marriage, but I'm afraid it won't work," to which I would say, "Don't listen to the fear. Don't listen to the anxiety. Listen to your hope. Listen to what you want."

Let's get the knowledge, decide on action, and then move beyond the fear to start tackling the real issues. Courage is not waiting for the fear to abate; it's not waiting for the fear to dissipate; it is not waiting for it to disappear. It's choosing to move forward, even when you're fearful. So courage is that place where we say, "You know what? It may not work, but it's worth the risk. I'm going to move forward. I've got to take that risk to get to what I want."

This is true everywhere in life. When I look around at what makes a difference between people who get somewhere interesting and those who don't, the difference is courage. It's not a lack of fear. The people who move forward had fear; they set it aside. When I created my System some years back, I had to really screw down my fear and say, "You know what? I am going to put this out there and see what people think. I am going to put it out into the world and see if it's useful. People might say mean things (and by the way, over the 12 years that I've been doing this now, lots of people have been happy to tell me mean things). But I can't let that stop me, because I have something to say." I have a message I want to share.

At some point, a person has to say, "My hopes are bigger than my fears, and I'm going to focus on that."

You have to have courage to keep yourself from being immobilized and to keep yourself from not reacting out of fear. Fear is a horrible motivator and is terrible at giving you direction. Fear points you to awful places. It causes you to be reactive, and then it gets you moving in the wrong direction. You would do well to think of your fear as just being a really crummy GPS system. It will tell you where to go — it is just that it is not a good way to get there and is probably not even a good place to go. So don't rely on that horrible GPS system. Rely on your courage, your hopes, your aspirations — those will get you to a better place.

What Next?

Where are you at a deficit today? Do you not have enough knowledge. Find the information you need, but not so much information that you are overwhelmed. Find just enough information that you know you have the knowledge base there.

Are you not taking action? What traps you? If you do not know what action to take, I will be providing some of that information here. You can find more in my System. If you are ready for someone to help you find the path, I do have a staff of Relationship Coaches who can point you in the right direction. Contact me and we can get that set up.

If your deficit feels like courage, remember this: courage is not something you gain. It is something you create. It is choosing to take action, in spite of how you are feeling (fear, in particular). Don't wait on courage to arrive. Decide to be courageous.

Now, let's look at some ways that you get in the way of yourself — and how to get out of your own way!

CHAPTER 6
YOUR LIMITING BELIEFS

"What can I do?" cried Sharon, "I can't do anything! I don't even know where to start! I want to save my marriage, but he refuses to even think about it." And with that, Sharon launched into a discussion that lasted at least 25 minutes, telling me why nothing could be done, why her marriage was a lost cause, and how she was useless.

After several attempts to slow down the avalanche of hopelessness, I finally got Sharon's attention: "Okay, so there is nothing you can do. You feel helpless. And you believe that your marriage is over. Is that correct?" I asked. Sharon, looking out through tearful eyes, blurted "Yes! It is useless!"

"Then why are you here?" I implored. "You know I work to help people save their marriages. So my guess is you have some hope."

"Hope? No. Maybe wishful thinking," Sharon replied.

"Well," I noted, "your first problem IS your thinking, but it is not particularly wishful. You already have placed limits on yourself. You have very limiting beliefs. And that is your first problem."

Sharon had no idea what a limiting belief is and had less understanding of why it matters. So I explained.

What are Limiting Beliefs?

Below our conscious thinking, we have a built-in group of beliefs that actually form and create our thoughts. They are filters that allow us to see the world in certain ways and blind us to seeing the world in other ways. Our built-in beliefs flavor our daily lives, our thoughts, and our actions in ways that we are only slightly aware.

Once we have these beliefs, we spend a great deal of our time unconsciously attempting to prove them correct. In fact, we refuse to see evidence to the contrary. This bias toward confirming our beliefs that we already hold is why we get stuck in them.

These beliefs can be aspirational or fearful. They can be freeing or restraining. Some beliefs show possibilities and some show limitations. Most are only partially correct or entirely false. Your beliefs about how to save your marriage are usually limiting.

Our fearful beliefs are powerful, and dangerous, for one important reason: they operate invisibly -- at least until we identify and name them. These same beliefs lose their power when daylight is cast upon them. When they can be examined, they evaporate.

Aspirational beliefs, on the other hand, grow stronger by being seen in the light of day. They begin to move us in stronger and more powerful ways when they are understood and embraced. So bringing fearful beliefs into the open destroys them and bringing aspirational beliefs into the open strengthens them. Which raises the question of why we don't bring them into the open more often?

First, many people fail to notice these beliefs in operation. Second, we have to poke around a bit in areas that make us fearful.

We mostly try to avoid the experience of fear. So, when we get near to something that makes us fearful, we move away from it. Our brain is trained to think that if something scares us, it is a threat. If it is a threat, there is danger. If there is danger, we should avoid it. Something triggers some fearful emotion and we naturally pull back in a defensive response. And we try to avoid feeling it again.

But if you want to save your marriage, you need to examine those fearful beliefs and let them go. The fear is not a true threat, but a warning that you are touching a deeply held belief. These beliefs, though, do not serve you!

Think of the limiting beliefs as chains that keep you stuck to the ground, bound to one place. Think of your aspirational beliefs as freeing -- cutting the chains to allow you to fly! They allow you to shift to new places and new possibilities.

Where Do Limiting Beliefs Come From?

Our limiting beliefs are built over a lifetime. It is a result of what we witnessed with our caretakers, how we were loved and cared for, how our siblings and friends related to us and we to them, and how other relationships in our lives have progressed.

Here is the interesting thing, and it is very important to know: Our Aspirational Beliefs and our Limiting Beliefs (fear-based) are mirror images of each other!

What you most hope for and what you most fear — mirror images. You may, for example, hope for a loving and caring, well-connected marriage. What you fear, then, is a marriage that is unloving, uncaring, and disconnected.

This next point is equally important: When that Limiting Belief is made conscious and examined, the Aspirational Belief grows and the Limiting Belief dims. It's as if the negative side of the mirror steams over and cannot be seen anymore.

In other words, when you move from fear – based beliefs to aspirational beliefs, you gain power and momentum. If you stay locked in the fear-based beliefs, you will be limited and controlled by them.

Limiting beliefs fall apart when examined because they are false. They are just fiction we have made up. But, aspirational beliefs are goals, targets, and hopes. We can move toward them, when we give up the fiction. You must remember that many pieces of fiction are "based on a real story." The events you recall that may have shaped your beliefs did happen. It is just that your beliefs built from those events stretch the actual events until they become fiction.

Our capacity to recall an event in accurate detail, knowing the internal reasons and motivations of those around us, is incredibly small. We are just not capable of understanding why people did what they did, which leaves us assigning blame to others, while removing our own responsibility and actions in the process.

Why Limiting Beliefs Can Sabotage Your Efforts To Save Your Marriage

If you want to save your marriage, you need to be much clearer about your limiting beliefs. For example, if your limiting belief is that someone cannot truly love you, you will unconsciously rebuff the attempts of somebody trying to love you. Over time, the other person will tire of trying to prove his/her love. This makes it even harder to save your marriage, as your spouse has become frustrated with the process.

Or what if you say you want to save your marriage, but you do not believe your marriage can be saved. Your actions to save your marriage will be short-lived. You will take some action to save your marriage, become frustrated, reinforce your belief, and give up on your efforts to save your marriage.

In other words, your limiting beliefs will both sabotage attaining the marriage you want and work against your efforts to save your marriage.

Your efforts to save your marriage are at least partially controlled by the beliefs that you hold. Not entirely, as there is also the response of your spouse, and of your own actions. However, the reaction of your spouse, and your own actions are both influenced by your limiting beliefs. And you have no control over the actions of your spouse. So you want to focus on the one place you have control — yourself.

The good news is that you can do something about your beliefs, once you make them conscious, look at them carefully, refuse to retreat from your fear, and then choose to move toward your aspirational beliefs.

Those Pesky Limiting Beliefs

We have already established that your limiting beliefs come from your past. They are unprocessed fears that come as a result of incomplete and imperfect care that you received as a child and from incomplete relationships along the path of life.

These limiting beliefs arise when our emotions begin to overwhelm us. Instead of facing those emotions, particularly fear, we move away from the emotions and lock in those beliefs. We lock in the scars that are created. Unprocessed, fear becomes what we avoid. It is not even the avoidance of the circumstances that first created that scar, but avoiding feeling the emotion associated with that scar.

Fear is like that. We quickly move from being fearful of a situation to being fearful of feeling the fear again. Nobody likes to feel fear, and so we just avoid it. Unfortunately, those beliefs are just below the surface, and while we may not be able to easily verbalize them, they create the lens through which we see other situations. We learn a lesson, good or bad, from situations in our past, and then use that lesson to predict what will happen in the future. Unfortunately, predictions usually fall far off of reality.

One clue to a limiting belief is that it is usually based in absolutes. Whenever we make absolute statements, like "always" or "never," we are probably caught in a limiting belief. If you hear yourself say "my spouse always," or "my spouse never…," you are probably looking at a limiting belief. Likewise, if you say "I always," or "I never…," you are likely naming a limiting belief. In reality, there are few absolutes to people and their reactions.

In fact, one way of dealing with limiting beliefs is to look for exceptions to the belief. For example, if you say, "I never get the love I want," then you can consciously look for times when this is not the case. You can always find a time when you did get the love you want, which disproves your belief.

This tactic assumes that you are open to the possibility that your limited belief is false. Many people are unwilling to accept this possibility. When somebody is unwilling to accept the possibility that their belief is wrong, they are forever trapped by it. All I ask is that you be open to the possibility that your beliefs are 1) false and 2) limiting.

One painful realization for many people is that when we hold onto limiting beliefs, it often allows us to escape our own responsibility. By having a limited belief, we avoid responsibility for own lives.

If someone claims that a spouse is "always" a certain way, then it relieves that person of responsibility, since there is nothing that can be done when a spouse is always a certain way. If you believe something about yourself in an absolute sense, then it relieves you of the responsibility of trying to do anything different, of trying to make a change, of trying to move to a different level. If it is absolute, then it cannot be changed. If it cannot be changed, then there is nothing I can do.

The limiting beliefs not only limit our view of the situation and color our view of the other person, but they also serve to relieve us of any need to change. Sometimes, it feels safer to refuse to change than to take on the possibility of something new. We often refuse to change because 1) it requires us to accept responsibility, and 2) it places us in new situations, which can be uncomfortable.

Uncomfortable yet?

Let's look at a few limiting beliefs that many people hold. Remember that this is not an extensive list. It is just a list of a few common ones, meant to get you thinking about your own limiting beliefs.

• "Relationships that are meant to be should not be this much struggle."

This is a common limiting belief. We seem to think that anything that is useful is easy, anything that is right is problem free. We have the idea that if there's a problem, then there must be a 'wrongness" to the situation. That is a very limiting belief, and it is also false. Every relationship has struggles, and every relationship can grow from the struggles. In fact, relationships that avoid struggle also avoid growth and will quickly find themselves without the resources to deal with the difficulties of life.

To put it more bluntly, 100% of marriages have difficulties and struggles. It is not a question of whether there is a struggle, but how you will deal with that struggle. Will you just keep struggling? Will you just avoid the struggle? Or will you make a decision to solve the struggle, once and for all?

Imagine for a moment that you decide that you want to have a leaner, more muscular body. So you go to the gym, and exercise a little bit, and begin to think, "If I was meant to have a lean, muscular body, I wouldn't have to struggle at it." Imagine that this person believes that he can get into better shape, become leaner, and more muscular, without exercise and without changing what he eats. Most people would find this to be a ridiculous statement. And yet that's exactly the belief that we transfer to relationships when we believe that there should be no problem in a relationship.

• "You can't trust a man/woman."

Many people carry around this belief. It may be perpetuated by jokes, sitcoms, and popular media, but it is deeper rooted than that. Somewhere along the way, somebody either told you or suggested to you by actions, that one gender or the other was entirely untrustworthy. You may apply it to your spouse, or you may apply it to yourself. You may think your spouse is untrustworthy, or believe that you are untrustworthy. Either way, it will affect your actions and your trust. If you believe that your gender is not trustworthy, it certainly gives you permission to not be trustworthy, as that is "just the way things are." If you think a spouse is untrustworthy, you will constantly look for reasons to believe that.

Just to be clear, this belief is one of those absolutes. To believe that any one gender is entirely untrue or untrustworthy means that you always have to be guarded around that gender. You can't let your guard down. And you can't trust that it is safe to be vulnerable.

Here is the truth: both genders have plenty of people who can be trusted and plenty of people who cannot be trusted. Your spouse is not 100% trustworthy, and neither are you. Researchers have shown that all of us are dishonest throughout the day. That does not make us untrustworthy, but does point to the fact that we all fall short in this category. If the measurement is 100% trustworthy or 100% untrustworthy, that's the trouble. I firmly believe that we all have thoughts that pop into our heads that do not need to see the light of day, and that certainly do not need to be shared with a spouse. Generating thoughts is just what our mind does. That does not make us untrustworthy; we are just the possessors of minds that are capable of unhealthy and unhelpful thoughts.

- **"I don't deserve a good marriage."**

This limiting belief is based in our own sense of self-worth. Perhaps you watched parents who were unable to make a good marriage. Perhaps you grew up with people telling you that you were not worthy of love. Or perhaps you've just given up, because your relationship hasn't gone the way you wanted it to. Either way, I believe that everyone deserves a good marriage. More than that, I don't think it's about deserving a good marriage, as much as creating a good marriage. We could go into a long philosophical discussion about what anyone deserves, versus what anyone gets. But that would keep us stuck. Instead, I believe that we should all make the best of where we are and what we have. It's not about deserving, it's about creating something worthwhile, and something that is bigger than us, and beyond us. A good marriage is just that.

- **"My spouse can't/won't change."**

This is a biggie. I hear it all the time. People tell me about how they are changing their lives, and how they are working at the relationship, but that their spouse is incapable of change. Or that their spouse just refuses to change. I found this to sometimes be the case. Sometimes, a spouse has not seen the reason for change. Sometimes, a spouse has been exactly the same from day one. So, they are a little confused by the demands for them to be different.

But what amazes me is the capacity that we all have to change and grow. In fact, I think this is the hallmark of being a human. Unlike the animal kingdom that has a hard time adapting to the environment and responds out of either fear or predation, humans are capable of reasoning and thinking things through. Humans are capable of consciously deciding to grow and change. Humans are able to adapt to a situation by thinking through what the situation requires.

What I have noticed is that many spouses are not invested enough in the relationship at this point and are therefore resistant to change. Those same spouses are willing to learn more about a sport, a hobby, or their work. That tells me, in fact proves my point, that they are capable of change and growth. So the real issue is how to shift someone into a growth mindset within the relationship. This is all about the power of connection. We will talk about that later. For now, assume your spouse, and any person, is not only capable of changing, but actually designed to change and grow.

- **"We married for the wrong reasons."**

This is a limiting belief. It may not be an entirely false belief. It is, nonetheless, limiting. What I mean by that is that marriages come together for lots of reasons. Sometimes it is out of necessity, sometimes it is for love, sometimes it just makes sense, and sometimes we can't even put our fingers on why we got married. But when we assume that we married for all the wrong reasons, we give ourselves an "out." This is when a limiting belief removes our responsibility. Their reasoning is that if we got married for the wrong reasons, then we need to end the relationship. But we do lots of things for the wrong reasons, and then make the reasons right. Sometimes, we get into jobs for the wrong reason. But then we find something good about that job, learn the job, and become quite good at it. We can do the same with the marriage.

In reality, the question is not why you got married, but how do you grow your marriage? It is not about the reasons behind the wedding, but the choice to have a thriving marriage.

- **"I can't forgive what he/she did."**

This is a very powerful limiting belief. It underestimates the capacity of anyone to forgive. It also points to how incorrectly we understand forgiveness. First, let's clear up what forgiveness is about. This belief assumes that forgiveness is for the other person. When somebody says "I can't forgive them," they don't want to offer something to that person. They want to hold onto something and to hold it over the other person.

Here is the truth about forgiveness: forgiveness is for YOU, so that you do not have to carry around the pain caused by someone else's actions. It is to free you from the constraints of resentment and hurt. A by-product of that action may be the restoration of a relationship and may even allow the other person some freedom from his/her own feelings of guilt or shame. However, forgiveness serves to free the person that has been hurt.

That being the case, then it becomes a matter, not of "can't," but of "won't." The person holding this limiting belief is really saying "I won't forgive what he/she did." The switch of words also brings about a switch in responsibility. It is up to the injured person to decide whether or not to forgive, not whether the injured person can forgive or whether the other person "deserves" forgiveness.

Not forgiving someone continually ties us to the actions of another. It traps us there and fools us into believing that the other person is the issue. This becomes a limiting belief and a trap to further self- and relational-development.

Let me state something very important about forgiveness, given the many misconceptions about it. Forgiveness does not mean lack of consequences! Sometimes, someone does something to us, and there are necessary consequences to their behavior. We may guard against a recurrence of some specific event or we may separate ourselves from that person. But this is different than forgiveness.

Likewise, forgiveness is not about forgetting something. "Forgive and forget" is a myth. You may forgive and remember it differently, but you are unlikely to forget. And what I mean by "remember differently" is that in the process of forgiveness, we often come to see a person in a different light — one that gives them a bit more humanity and fallibility. Seeing someone differently can sometimes lead us to understand their actions differently.

Your Aspirational Beliefs

Limiting beliefs come from fear, linked to hurts and scars in our past. Aspirational beliefs come from a very different space. Your healthiest place, a more pure and true part of your psyche, holds onto what could be. These beliefs reflect our true values, not our fears. These beliefs give you direction and point you toward health/healing.

They are also, interestingly, often the mirror images of what we most fear. For example, in our list of limiting beliefs, I noted the belief, "I can't forgive what he/she did." An aspirational belief is "I am capable of forgiving, can forgive, and choose to forgive the hurt." Notice the difference in feel. Notice the change in space that comes from that belief.

These beliefs are aspirational because they are not necessarily completed. They are a source of direction and create a place of "becoming." In the example above, forgiveness is not a point-in-time. It is a process. It is a re-understanding of what happened and who the other person is. You see, built into a refusal to forgive is the belief that the other person does not deserve to be seen as anything other than flawed.

But I have a counter-belief that I hold dear: "People do the best they can, where they are." This is not an assertion that everyone is operating at an optimal level, only that people are doing the best they can in the point-in-space where they find themselves. We all have places where we do not live up to what we could/should be doing. But when we fall short, it does not negate the fact that we all are still trying the best we can.

In fact, that very belief: "People do the best they can, where they are," is aspirational. It seeks to see people through a different lens than that of judgment. We are all growing and becoming. So the best I did yesterday may not be the best I do next week. The path of growing and becoming means we can always do better — but we are doing the best we can, where we are right now.

Between Aspiration and Fear

Our beliefs that are based in fear are, for the most part, fiction.

They are often fictionalized accounts of fact. But they are still fiction. In the list of limiting beliefs above, all are pieces of fiction. We use them to write a story that may be interesting and entertaining (and perhaps quite dramatic), but does nothing to serve us. Behind the lie that these beliefs are protecting us is the truth that they are also relieving us of responsibility. And they limit our potentials of life and relationship.

Aspirational beliefs provide us direction. They can point the way to growth and to greater connection. Fortunately, we can choose to adopt aspirational beliefs. Even if we do not fully believe and live them right now, we can move toward that new belief. But limiting beliefs are those that we have carried with us from long ago. Often, they are rooted in our childlike thinking that is only focused on what seems to be self-preservation. It is really self-limitation, but we are not always good at seeing the difference.

Remember, both limiting and aspirational beliefs are originally unconscious to us. They operate as fact and encourage us to find further information to prove the belief true. This is especially true of the fear-based limiting beliefs. Our belief system is caught between safety and opportunity. But fear is always rooted in safety. Growth is always rooted in opportunity.

Our existence in this place-in-time is due to the fact that our ancestors were safety-minded. For those who took too many risks in an unsafe environment, their gene pool was eliminated. That creates in us an overly-sensitive "early warning system" that runs on fear. We are wired to be overly cautious and fearful, even though our environment is no longer as unsafe as the environment that created that system.

We are left with an alarm system that goes off when it spots a shadow of a possibility that something might be amiss. Instead of waiting to assess the real threat, this system sounds the alarm and writes an account of what is going to happen, even if the account is false and overblown.

Sometimes, our alarm system leads us to always look for the disaster that might happen instead of the recovery that could happen. We become focused only on the pain of the situation, not the potential.

Our alarm system can even stop us from starting a process of saving a marriage. On a weekly basis, I receive letters from people who tell me they want to save their relationship, but they don't want to get started. Why don't they want to start? Because what if it doesn't work? What if their efforts fail? What if their spouse refuses to stay in the relationship?

In other words, they make a decision to do nothing because there is a possibility that nothing will work. They choose to stay frozen in inaction because they fear that action may not work. Many are surprised when I point out that doing nothing absolutely guarantees that the marriage will not be saved. Taking no action certainly proves that the marriage could not be saved. But it never proves that doing something would have been fruitless. It never proves that perhaps the marriage could be saved.

Your Turn:

So what are YOUR limiting beliefs? What are the pieces of fiction that you carry around — even if they are based on real events — that keep you from moving forward with your marriage and your life?

1) Make a list of all the reasons you CAN'T save your marriage. What reasons, about you, your relationship, your spouse, or whatever else, keep you from saving your marriage?

2) Now, begin to examine that list. Are there exceptions to that list? Can you prove the reason incorrect? Can you at least consider that the reason is incorrect, and that there is a possibility of doing something? (By the way, I know that you think something can be done for one very simple reason: you are reading this book!)

3) Next, let's flip each of the reasons to an aspiration. Just move it to the "possible." For example, if you wrote, "My spouse will never change," rewrite that to "My spouse is capable of change." You don't have to believe it right now. I just want you to see it. If you wrote, "Our marriage has always been disconnected," rewrite it to "Our marriage can be connected and satisfying." Again, you don't have to believe it. Just rewrite it.

4) Choose to let go of the limiting beliefs you listed. But re-read, on a daily basis, your list of aspirational beliefs. They will begin to be more activated than the limiting beliefs, and you will begin to move

toward actions that activate the possibilities.

Notice any negative reaction you have to whether this exercise will work or not. Then accept that you may have just stumbled onto another limiting belief! Then make sure you go through the exercise above. It will help as we turn our attention to changing limiting beliefs in the next few pages.

Changing Limiting Beliefs

As we have just noted, we all carry around with us, every one of us, limiting beliefs. We have limiting beliefs about what we think is possible. We have limiting beliefs about what we know as realities. We have limiting beliefs, and when I say limiting beliefs, I mean that these beliefs close us down.

Limiting beliefs are always based in fear and sometimes are used as a way of relieving us of responsibility. If I say to myself, "I can't save this marriage; there is nothing I can do to save this marriage," then at that moment, I've already decided that there's nothing I can do. I remove the responsibility for myself to take any action whatsoever. And so limiting beliefs sometimes let us off the hook and allow us to sidestep responsibility. Limiting beliefs also keep us from taking action, because "What's the point?" The belief limits what we think is possible, so 1) it limits our responses and 2) it limits our responsibility. When that happens, the correlation between limiting our responses and limiting our responsibility keeps us stuck.

So one of the important starting point in this process is to identify what limiting beliefs you carry around with you. And we all have different limiting beliefs.

There are some general guidelines about these beliefs. They are usually statements like: "I can't," "They won't," "We won't be able to. . . ," or similar types of statements. Sometimes, it's also about the kind of person you are or about the kind of person your spouse is that limits your belief.

When I have people come in and tell me that there's something wrong at the core with their spouse, they've limited what can happen because they have already discounted the other person. They've already eliminated the possibility that there is somewhere that they can move to, instead of seeing that there is a pattern going on between the two people, an interactive pattern for which there are new possibilities, new ways that it can move when the possibility of change is embraced.

We tend to look at the "end result" of where the other person is, but take note of the "process" when we look at ourselves. We assign a description to the other person: "My spouse is always angry," "My spouse refuses to connect," "My spouse won't listen to me," which is about a point-in-time. When we look inward, though, we notice what got us here, the process: "After all of this, I have no choice but to be angry and hurt," "I have tried to connect so many times, so it is useless," "When my spouse keeps bringing up the same issues, I just have to start ignoring them."

Yet both people have both elements. Both of you have a current attitude, and both of you have a process that got you there. Limiting beliefs keep us from truly noting one or the other. But since beliefs are just that, beliefs — not truths, we can challenge and change them

I want to spend just a little time examining how we change those limiting beliefs. We all have them, so we can all use the information on how to change limiting beliefs, not just about marriage but about life.

There are four steps to changing your limiting beliefs, which I call the 4C's of changing limiting beliefs.

4 C's of Changing Limiting Beliefs

1) C-onscious. In order to change a belief, you need to become conscious of the limiting belief and become fully aware of it, allowing yourself to identify it. That's the first step: you have to be able to recognize what it is. So when you find yourself with statements of absolutes: "I can't do this." "I won't do this." — you have likely landed on a limiting belief.

Notice that there's a negative tone to most limiting beliefs: "My spouse is always this way." "My spouse is never this way." "Things are always this way." "Things are never this way." "Marriages never work out." Such negative and absolute statements are indicators of a limiting belief. "My spouse is always going to (fill in the blank)" is a limiting belief. "I can't gain any traction in this" is a limiting belief.

So the first thing is to become conscious of that negativity. What are the places where you have those limits? Here's the cool thing: you're here because you are already one step past the "There is nothing that can be done" limiting belief. The people who really,

really have embraced the limiting belief that "Nothing can be done to save my marriage," don't seek information, don't look for help, and don't take action. The fact that you are here tells me that such a belief is either only partially held by you or not held by you at all.

But I want you to always be thinking, "What are my limiting beliefs?" You want to make them conscious, and the reason is because they operate below the level of consciousness for most of the time. They lurk just below the surface. They are constantly rear-ending us but they lurk just below the surface. When we bring them out, when we look at them, when we bring them to the surface, we have a target. And the reason we are going to use that as a target is because we are going to counteract it. We are going to find a way, once we've made it conscious, to move past it.

Identifying those limiting beliefs was Step 1 in the exercise at the end of the last section. You completed that, right?

Which brings us to step two:

2) C-hallenge the belief. The way you challenge the belief is to look for evidence of the opposite. For instance, if you have a belief from your family or from somewhere else that "Marriages never work out," I want you to look around and notice the marriages that do work out. I want you to notice the marriages that are happy and content. I know that many will say, "But you never know what's happening behind closed doors," and that's true. Some marriages that look happy end up being a facade.

But marriages do work out. In fact, let's just go with statistics. If you have a belief system that says "Marriages never work out," understand that a little better than 50% of the time, they do work out. Then you have to say, "Okay, better than one out of two marriages does work out. That goes against my basic belief that none work out." You could have a belief that every marriage works out and go through life that way, but that's a little hard to hold onto. Usually, our beliefs are more toward the negative and are limiting. So if you have the belief that marriages never work out, I want you to just take a look around and see that marriages do work out.

Think about how to challenge your other beliefs: "I can't get my spouse to change," for example. I want you to think back to the times that maybe that wasn't true. Because you can always find a place where that wasn't true: "Oh, I helped him/her change in that way." Or what about the belief that that you might carry around that you never get the love you need? Just for a moment, think of the times when you did get the love you needed.

You are trying to challenge the belief. So first, you become conscious of the belief. Then second, you challenge the belief and prove that there are times when it's been wrong. If there is a time when a limiting belief based in absolutes has been wrong, then that belief is false. You can no longer say "never" or "always."

That was Step 2 in the exercise at the end of the last chapter. You have already had an experience of doing this!

3) C-hange your perspective. Next, I want you make a change in perspective. Reverse your belief. Instead of holding onto the limiting belief that marriages never work out — and you don't have to change to "Marriages always work out," because that gets us to another absolute — but there's a midpoint in saying "Marriages can and do work out," "Marriages can be fulfilling," "I can get the love I want." Notice that we don't want to be captured by an absolute. If your belief system is "I never get the love I want," you don't want to flip it to "I always get the love I want," because that's not true for any of us. But "I can get the love I want," that's a shift you want to make.

You want to be conscious of your belief. Then challenge that belief; find evidence of the contrary. Then change the belief by changing your perspective. Many times all that is necessary is to change the negative statement to a possibility statement: "Marriages never work out" to "Marriages can work out." That's a possibility.

That was Step 3 in the exercise at the end of the last chapter. So you already know how to do this, too!

4) C-ommit to the new belief. You solidify your new belief by committing to the new belief. For example, "There's nothing I can do in the marriage" — that's an absolute. "I can do some things to improve my marriage" — that's a possibility. Now commit to working on that new belief.

Notice the process that we are going through is to first become aware of what's going on, and then to solidify a belief that is counter to that. So you become conscious of your belief. Then you challenge that belief by looking for evidence to the contrary. Then you change your perspective by stating that belief in the positive, in the world of possibility. Then you solidify the new belief by committing to your new belief and you start looking for evidence of that new belief.

When you start looking for evidence of when it happens, you will be just as successful at finding evidence of the new belief as when you were looking for evidence of the negative — of the absolute limiting belief. Whatever belief we hold, we will find evidence to support it. We will find proof that supports any belief because we stop looking at the evidence that runs contrary to that belief. With limiting beliefs, just being open to evidence to the contrary begins a shift away from the limiting belief.

So the Four C's of changing limiting beliefs, anywhere in life, are: become **Conscious** — conscious of the belief. **Challenge** — challenge the belief. **Change** — change your perspective by making a possibility belief. And **Commit** — commit to the change by seeking evidence to support it. When you do these four steps, you will find that you can take on any limiting belief, turn it around and move it to something else, something more powerful. So now, continue looking for those limiting beliefs around your marriage relationship — and in your life.

CHAPTER 7
THE 3 C'S OF SAVING YOUR MARRIAGE

"So, how DO you save your marriage?" asked the frustrated voice on the other end of the call. "Eric" had been working to save his marriage for some time. And it seemed that no matter where he looked, all he saw was conflicting advice: "fix your communication," "make her jealous," "use reverse psychology," and lots of other "gems" out there. But it left Eric no closer to saving his marriage than when he started. "Why is it so hard?," wondered Eric. I had to agree. Since I created SaveTheMarriage.com, there has been an avalanche of information out there. It is almost too much. Pretty quickly, you get overwhelmed and feel like giving up.

But just for a moment, imagine that it is not a difficult process. In fact, imagine for a moment that the process is actually quite simple. Like many things, we tend to complicate things. Often, unnecessarily. In fact, almost always unnecessarily.

There are only three elements that must be addressed in your efforts to save your marriage. But I must warn you, there are three major elements that must be addressed! Each element is crucial and creates an intertwined effort. These elements are the steps to saving a marriage. The elements are necessary parts of any relationship, and until they are addressed, your marriage will have vulnerabilities.

Every marriage needs 1) connection between the partners, 2) individual growth of the partners, and 3) a direction for the relationship. Those are the ingredients of a successful marriage. So when a marriage is in trouble, these elemental pieces can be addressed and activated. The necessary elements become the necessary steps in saving your marriage.

Let's take a quick look at each step. Then we will go into each step in-depth.

C-onnect

The simple truth is that marriage relationships become stressed and troubled by a lack of connection. We humans are designed for connection. And when we do not get the connection we need, we feel like we are starving for attention.

And the longer the disconnection goes on, the more a relationship suffers. A feeling of distance becomes a feeling of disdain — all from disconnection.

But the path back is simply rebuilding the connection. In fact, the heart of reviving the relationship is just that: reconnection.

The problem is that you are likely out of practice, perhaps a bit angry, and feeling hurt, yourself. None of that leaves you wanting to reconnect. Yet this is the way out of the mess. Connection revives the marriage. Continued disconnection starves and strangles the marriage.

It is at about this point in my conversations when people say "What about me? Why doesn't my spouse have to reconnect with me?"

The answer I give is far more pragmatic than fair: "You are the one who is with me and who is working on saving your marriage. So for right now, focus on reconnecting. When you reconnect, your spouse will eventually follow."

If you are working to save your marriage, at least for the time-being, you have to set aside your own wishes and hopes for connection coming your way. Focus on providing connection. Practically speaking, someone has to take action. Take on the task of reconnecting.

C-hange Yourself

Just like Eric, on the other end of the phone line, you are somebody I do not know. So whatever I say, please do not take it personally. Instead, it is based on nearly a quarter of a century of helping couples. I know from experience what needs to happen, even if I don't know you.

So, Step 2 in saving your marriage is to change yourself. Grow and develop into a higher caliber person. . . regardless of where you are now.

Let's be honest: we all have places where we can improve and grow. We all have places where we are not maximizing our potential, where we are not "showing up."

Something happens to all of us when we "settle down." We stop growing and developing. And as we do this, we begin to lose ground. Eventually, if someone is not careful, the attractiveness that our spouse once felt begins to wane. We slowly move toward a state of stagnation.

It is at about this time that some people start screaming, "But why should I have to keep trying to attract my spouse? Why can't my spouse just love me?" Again, a good philosophical question. But I am a practical man. Practically speaking, if you are trying to save your marriage, you want to become more and more attractive to your spouse — not less. Simple pragmatism.

Unfortunately, our philosophical side can kick and scream and demand that "It's not fair." But then, for a moment, notice that the philosophical side is really just that child's voice crying out about unfairness. And as my parents used to tell me, "Life is not always fair."

So, back to the task. In the process to save your marriage, you will want to change yourself. Grow. Develop. Become more of what you know you need to become. In the end, you will be more satisfied with life. And the more satisfied you are, the better your chances of saving the marriage. You become, in the process, more attractive to your spouse and to yourself.

Step 2 in saving your marriage is to Change Yourself.

C-reate A New Path

Marriages fail because couples disconnect. Marriages fail because individuals stop growing. And finally, marriages fail because the individuals that make up the couple never knew where they were headed.

So the final step is to create a new path. Imagine where your marriage could head, and what your marriage could be. Don't just ponder it for a moment, but really consider it.

I deeply believe we do a great disservice to couples when they marry. We spend lots of money, time, effort, and energy into celebrating a short wedding service — then we send the couple out into the world, congratulating them and wishing them the best. . . but without telling the couple about what they are trying to do. We don't let them know the truth about what a marriage is. There is no clear goal toward which they can head. "Have a great life together" doesn't cut it.

It is like sending a couple out on a trip with a GPS, and then forgetting to tell them what address to put into the GPS system. They can wander around, but if they do not know the destination, they are unlikely to find their way, and certainly unlikely to get there with any efficiency.

So what is the destination? Being a WE. At the point of marriage, two people are trying to form a team, a unit — a WE, as I describe it. But if a couple does not know this is the goal, how are they ever going to get there?

"You and Me" is the start of a relationship. But if a couple does not understand and does not get to "WE," then they will eventually drift into "You versus Me." Destruction of the relationship follows, for the simple reason that nobody knew better.

One of my central attempts in my material on how to save your marriage is how to build the relationship and how to become a WE. It is a roadmap to becoming a team

Save your marriage by following these 3 steps.

That's it. That's all you need to focus upon as you work to save your marriage. Follow those three steps, and you can save your marriage, even if you are the only one that wants to work on it! Let's get started!

CHAPTER 8
C-ONNECT WITH YOUR SPOUSE

Many people ask me what the core strength of any marriage is. That strength is connection. In fact, without connection, the relationship cannot survive. I don't say that from a philosophical standpoint but a practical standpoint. In fact, science would back this up. While marriage is not just about a feeling of connection, it is the glue of any relationship.

Many couples have strong marriages without common interests, common political views, common styles of interacting, or even similar backgrounds. What they do share is a strong sense of connection.

In fact, I would argue that connection is at the root of "falling in love." It is a basic human need. But it is a need that we often underestimate, undervalue, and misunderstand. If you don't have it, your marriage will eventually wither and die, as both people begin to seek connection in other ways outside of the relationship. Some people find it in work, some people find it in hobbies, and some people find it in another person.

Think back to how your relationship started. If it's like most relationships, it began with two people noticing each other. For some reason, each felt something different about the other person, something different than they felt about their friends or other acquaintances. Perhaps it was something different than any other person of romantic interest in the past. So, they began to get to know each other better. They did things together, shared things together.

Slowly, each person reached out in some way that was then reciprocated by the other person. This included physical affection, gifts, attention, words of encouragement, desires for more time together, and any other number of ways of reaching out. This begins an upward cascade of feelings of attachment. The more attachment there is, the stronger the emotions between the two people. Eventually, the couple goes from "being in like," to "being in love." (This is the upward arc of the trajectory of a marriage we discussed earlier.)

The path may not have necessarily included finding common interests; it was instead focused on connection. It was a connection that nurtured each other, and deepened the feelings, the trust, and the desire to be together. Is that something similar to the path you and your spouse followed?

As we have seen, the path of destruction in a relationship is a mirror image of the path of connection. How people fall apart in a relationship is the exact opposite of how they come together in a relationship.

The initial connection in any relationship can shift to disconnection. At some point, the attraction that pulled a couple together is the repelling that pushes them apart. Connection is so central to the relationship that if it is missing, the relationship will be unsatisfying and ultimately unsustainable.

The Science of Connection

It is only been in the last half-century or so that scientists have understood how important connection is to humans. This, in spite of the fact that humans have always needed this connection. Biological, psychological, and spiritual connection — it is literally wired into our brains, our bodies, and our minds.

When I was in a psychology class, I remember an experiment that still haunts me. The scientists removed a baby monkey from the mother. They were kept separated. (That feeling you have right now, in your gut, about how mean that is. . . that is you identifying with the loss of connection.)

The baby monkey was given a choice between two new "mothers," both made of wire. One held a bottle, but was just cold, bare wire. The other had no food, but had open, warm, and soft arms, the wire being covered with terry cloth and warmed.

In the movies I have seen of this experiment, that baby monkey chose the warm-but-nutritionless mother over the food-but-cold-wire mother, every time. The monkey chose this to the point of starving itself. The baby monkey was seeking connection over nourishment.

Humans are like that monkey. We need that connection. In fact, we have greater needs for connection. As far as we know it, monkeys do not sit around talking about their aspirations and dreams. Monkeys do not talk about memories and expectations that they have. In other words, the human capacity for language has also increased our need for this connection. It has expanded the ways that we can be connected, but it has also increased our need for that connection.

Researchers have clearly demonstrated that this connection, human to human, is what bonds parents and children. That has been known for some time. But the newer realization is that this need for connection is at the heart of the marital relationship. The marital relationship is not simply a relationship of survival, but is also one of aspiration. Again, this is a point that shifts the human relationship away from any other type of relationship in the animal kingdom. Humans have more potential than just survival. The need for survival, of staying together to survive, to raise children, to pull together the necessary elements of living, that's just the baseline for marriage.

We humans need something more than this. This is why our aspirational beliefs are so important. These aspirations are what bring us to higher levels of connection. It's what we look for. It's what we seek out.

I have never had someone tell me that when they were looking for a spouse, what they were looking for was a "person to survive with me." I do hear individuals talk about finding someone who will enjoy their pursuits, travel with them, do amazing things, and aspire to a higher life. Our ideal of a spouse is no longer a good hunter/gatherer. It is someone who will be our companion for life.

This is the power of connection: it either makes a marriage or holds it back.

We live in a society where many marriages are connection-starved. Spouses feel the absence of connection and the pain of that absence. They feel starved for something more. You can think of the connection as food.

There are three major "food groups" to connection: physical, emotional, and spiritual. These three "food groups" are all necessary for a balanced diet of connection and the marriage. Just like the necessary food groups for our bodies, when one is missing, our body can get out of balance. When all are lacking, a body will fall apart.

If we cannot get the food we need, we feel the physical pain of hunger. Over time, that feeling of hunger calls us to seek out any way of addressing it. The same is true for marriage. When the marriage is starved for connection, each person will begin to look for this connection somewhere. It may come from our children, our job, our hobbies, or somebody else. But we will seek out this connection, as an attempt to bring in what is missing from our bodies.

Here are some symptoms of too little connection:

1. Disconnection. This is the feeling of distance, of being out of sync, and of not having a sense of being a team with a spouse. This is an early symptom of a lack of connection. It is really just the feeling of disconnection, that spot of realizing that what you're wanting in a relationship is just not there. It is the vague understanding that something is missing and that you're not a team. This symptom can come and go in otherwise healthy relationships. And at the point when this is the only symptom, it's easy to solve by simply reconnecting. Couples often try doing things like finding a new hobby together, going on date nights together, or reading a book together. What is behind any of these attempts is really an attempt at growing the connection. Unfortunately, many couples have moved beyond the symptom before they do anything.

2. Disinterest. After feeling disconnected and not having this issue solved, one person may begin to lose interest in connecting. Starving for connection, a person can begin to lose some strength. This disinterest may show itself as refusing to participate in previous activities or refusing to cheer on the other person's interests. Hobbies and activities are seen as threats to the relationship; they are no longer supported, but resisted.

3. Disregard. After losing interest, the couple begins to disregard each other. They don't take each other into account and begin to work from a more individual pattern. This is not the same as each having individual interests. This is when one or both choose to act on their own, without considering the impact on the other person. They may choose to do activities, not just separately, but without consulting with their spouse.

4. Disrespect. As each person begins to disregard the other person and his/her feelings, the level of respect begins to fall. Over time, each treats the other in less and less civil ways. The disrespect shows in caustic comments, passive-aggressive or aggressive behavior, lack of cooperation, and an unwillingness to find a mutual solution to any matter. Criticism of each other grows, and others are often pulled into the conflict as a verification of each that he/she is "right."

5. Disappointment. As the disconnection grows, the symptom of disappointment emerges. It really is a matter of disillusionment. One or both realize that their expectations of what a marriage might be are colliding with what the marriage has become. In other words, they began to see that they are not going to get what they want out of the marriage. The disappointment begins to be fueled by frustration. At this point, the couple may stop even trying to work on change. This is often the point when a couple begins to play the "blame game." Both point the finger at the other person for what is missing. Blaming quickly cascades into a focus on the problems of the other person and the blamelessness of the self. Each person begins to self-justify his/her actions as warranted, given the other person's problems.

6. Dislike. While each may, at this point, still feel love and concern for the other, each generally has feelings of dislike for the other. Each dislikes being around the other, doesn't enjoy the other's presence, and sees less and less good in the other person. In fact, this symptom is marked by both people focusing on the negative traits of the other person. Likely, these traits have always been there. But they have always been outweighed by the feelings of attraction and connection. When those feelings go missing, what is left are the shortcomings that we all have. The shortcomings begin to be the focus of thoughts and arguments. And the shortcomings begin to build a new story of who the other person is. It is always a story of deficit.

7. Disdain. Feelings of dislike grow, and the stories of the short-fallings of the spouse begin to increase. Before, the issue was merely disliking them. Now, the dislike is mixed with anger and resentment. Disdain is what emerges. This strong feeling of being repelled by the other person begins to collapse the commitments made to the other person. At this point, the marriage crisis has deepened, if the marriage hasn't already ended.

Three Types of Connection — The Connection Food Groups

Marriages need nourishment. That nourishment is connection. Three major "food groups" of connection provide the nourishment. All three are important. However, just like our eating habits, we don't necessarily have or require a balanced diet. Sometimes, one is more important and more available than another. But over time, optimal health comes from a diet that includes all three.

If one area of connection is less available, having the other two helps to sustain the deficit. At a minimum, one area is necessary, just to stave off *connection starvation.*

The three "food groups" of connection are Physical Connection, Emotional Connection, and Spiritual Connection.

Physical Connection

Contrary to some people's assumptions, physical connection is not just about sex. It certainly includes the sexual connection, but is not limited to that. Unfortunately, when this area of connection is low or missing, sex is both what is craved and what is scapegoated.

Physical connection includes sex, but also includes all other variations of touch: snuggling, hugging, holding, caressing, back rubbing, kissing, holding hands, and any other non-aggressive physical contact.

This physical connection is the most primal of all connections. We are born into the world of physical connection. From our earliest moments, we learn to associate physical contact with either safety and warmth or threat and danger. In healthy families, we learn to calm down when there is physical connection —when we are held and cuddled. In more dysfunctional families, the anxiety of the family system can be transferred to the child, and physical connection can feel more threatening than soothing. But even in those situations, children seek out the connection and attention of physical touch.

Our biological systems are primed for this physical connection. Remember that monkey experiment? That baby monkey would give up sustenance for a feeling of nurturance. The trade was warmth and softness for food. This was true, even to the point of starvation. The need for physical touch is deeply ingrained.

When you touch or are touched, the hormone oxytocin is released into your system. This hormone is a naturally calming chemical that sends a signal to the brain that "all is well." Remember that calming feeling of holding a small baby against you? That physical feeling was facilitated by oxytocin.

That same chemical is secreted whenever there is more than a brush of physical affection. A hug of more than a few seconds causes it to be excreted. Sex causes a huge release of the hormone. And that hormone leads to a feeling of bonding with whomever that contact triggered the release. To have this effect, the touch has to be affectionate and non-aggressive. The effect of this physical touch is deeply bonding and connecting.

When I am teaching SCUBA diving, we stress that in emergency situations, you immediately establish physical contact with your dive partner. This is both to make sure you are together through the crisis and to establish the calming of the physical contact. Anxiety is combated by the physical connection and the natural release of oxytocin. Again, think back to an upset baby. Calming is done by touching and holding. The process is automatic and wired into our biology.

Emotional Connection

When I speak with couples before they get married, I ask them to tell me about the strengths of their relationship. Invariably, they talk about emotional support for each other. When one has a bad day, the other cheers them up. When one is anxious and frustrated, the other provides support and perspective. When the struggles of life come along, strong relationships provide emotional support for the couple. They support each other.

Emotional connection is about support — the feeling of being supported. It is also about a sense of being heard and validated. Sometimes, it can seem that the whole world is against you. When you feel that someone else is always "in your corner," always "has your back," it is easier to face the struggles and frustrations that are an inevitable part of life.

So, emotional connection comes from, and is nurtured by, the sense that you each have the other's best interests, are supported by and supportive of the other, and are protective of each other.

In her book, *Hold Me Tight*, Sue Johnson suggests that this level of emotional connection is clarified by three questions:

1) Are you **accessible** when I try to reach out to you?
2) Will you be **responsive** to my needs?
3) Are you **engaged** in this relationship.

Accessible, Responsive, and Engaged can be remembered by the acronym, "A.R.E." This acronym provides the fundamental pieces of emotional connection in a relationship.

Being **accessible** is not just a matter of being available, of having a physical presence. It is more about being emotionally accessible. Are you paying attention to and interested in your spouse's thoughts and feelings? Can your spouse get your attention when he/she wants and needs it? Are you engaged in listening? This, in some ways, represents a choice in priorities. Do you set down whatever is occupying your attention to attend to your spouse? If so, you have demonstrated that your spouse is the priority, not the television, paper, or smartphone.

Being **responsive** means you work to identify and respond to the emotional elements of a conversation. Every conversation happens on two levels: the content level and process level. The content refers to what is said — the facts. The process refers to the underlying emotions and meanings. While there are many times when content is all that is necessary in a response, when it is between spouses, the process is crucial. "We never go out" can be argued on a content level by responding, "We went out just last week." What is missed on the process level is the emotional aspect: "I feel disconnected and want more time with you." That is not answered by a response to the content that argues the facts. It is answered on the emotional level, "It sounds like maybe we need to be a bit more intentional about spending time together. How about we go out together Saturday night?"

Being **engaged** is about being both emotionally present and connected. It is the sense that the two of you are in synch with each other and emotionally connected. This is not an absence of conflict, but that points of conflict are resolved and you both move ahead in the relationship. This engagement is more difficult for people to articulate, but it is a feeling of connection that feels secure and consistent.

Emotional connection is crucial in order for a couple to trust the process of working through difficulties and frustrations in the marriage. And let's be clear: even a very connected marriage is going to have difficulties and disagreements. That is built into the fabric of living so closely with someone. It is also built into any relationship where both of you have to find a common path forward, given a commitment to stay together for life.

Spiritual Connection

The layer of connection that is perhaps deepest and rarest is that of spiritual connection. The reason for this is because we often operate at a point that forgets this level of our lives in the day to day. In other words, when people lose their own connection with their spiritual life, they are not likely to be bringing it into their marriage.

Your spiritual life is not just about your religious beliefs. In fact, that is one of the reasons that many people lose touch with this area of life. They come to equate it with only their religious beliefs, locking that area of life into a very narrow area of existence.

But we all have a spiritual life, regardless of our religious beliefs. Our religious beliefs are one part of our spiritual existence, but only one facet.

Your internal life of meaning, purpose, hopes, dreams, and aspirations are all part of this spiritual life. The layer of your life that includes morality, justice, and connection with humanity and the universe is a part of your spiritual life.

How you make sense of life, your own life and the life of others, and how you make sense of what happens in your life and the lives of others — those are parts of your spiritual life. This includes your philosophy of life (we all have one) and beliefs about why things happen the way they do.

Often, we live in cultures, though, that leave us disconnected from the spiritual area of our lives. We often live our lives in the busyness and bustling of a world where we "have to get things done," and don't reflect much on these areas. Yet they still live within us, yearning for a hearing. Our spiritual life keeps calling to be heard, whether we are listening or not.

For most, this voice becomes louder and louder as life moves forward. Often, this is part of the reawakening that accompanies midlife. In fact, the midlife crisis is the reemergence of our spiritual life, practically demanding attention and a hearing.

Sometimes, couples awaken to this voice at different times. One person begins to have a stirring of his or her spiritual life, but the other is still in "life mode" or "survival mode." This can lead to deep divisions as one seeks more meaning and the other is still focused on the "have to do's" of daily life that can drown out the spiritual layer of life.

What, then, is Spiritual Connection? It is the level of connection that comes from sharing and knowing each other's deepest thoughts, beliefs, hopes, and dreams. This is a deep level of intimacy, to trust someone with the deep parts of your soul that are rarely shared with anyone. The deep connection is created because of how closely these areas of life are held.

Here is the irony: it is usually the sharing of these areas that lead couples to fall in love with each other. Think back to your own days of connecting — of falling in love. My guess is that part of what "cinched the deal" was your sharing of hopes and dreams. It probably also had some sense of connection about values and beliefs. You may have had common goals and aspirations, similar views on the world. These all represent your spiritual life. You connected over sharing this inner world. More than that, you connected over the sense you had that you could trust this other person with those most vulnerable points of life. What you held most dearly was likely guarded by this new love, and vice versa.

That is typically what I hear from couples who have become engaged. It was one of those markers that this relationship was different. They realized they could share parts of life that they had never been able to share before. They could talk for hours about their lives and where they wanted life to go. They could share not just the stories of what had happened to them, but how it had created who they are. In other words, each one guarded and treasured both the past events and future hopes that make us who we are.

Then what happens? We lose track of this and stop sharing. We start to lose track of what is most important to ourselves and to our spouse as it is crowded out by daily life. And suddenly, this part of life is disconnected from the relationship.

Then, the spiritual connection is either minimized or eliminated. And with that, the aspirational part of our lives is removed from the relationship. This means that there is less pulling us forward toward something greater, and more focus on fear — or avoiding fear.

Couples who maintain their spiritual connection stay in touch with their own internal lives and risk sharing them with the other person. Both being in touch and risk-sharing have to be happening. When someone loses touch with that inner world of importance, that person becomes lost and directionless. That person also has nothing to share with his or her spouse. Sharing that important area is also risking sharing a very intimate part of life. Taking the risk is the only path to establishing this spiritual connection. The process, though, starts with knowing your own inner world.

Are you attending to your own spiritual life? Are you in touch with what is meaningful and purposeful? Are you connected with your hopes, dreams, and aspirations? If so, you have a place from which to share. If not, you will want to attend to that for yourself.

Three Arenas of Connection

Okay, we have now outlined and noted the three important areas of connection — the "food" of the relationship. At this point, you understand the dynamics of physical, emotional, and spiritual connection. Notice that these three areas work from our most primitive and primal needs to much higher levels of living. In fact, the three areas actually match three specific layers of your brain.

Physical touch addresses the connections of the most primitive part of the brain — the part that is geared toward survival. This area is dominated by the Amygdala, which is focused only on looking for threats. It is responsible for our fearful reactions. Those insecure feelings and reactions we cannot even name sometimes — they originate here.

Emotional connection comes from the Limbic System of the brain. This part of the brain is the part wired for communal living and support. It adds emotions onto our survival instincts. A point midway between fear and aspiration, it contains our emotional life and feeds in both directions.

Spiritual connection comes from our Neo-Cortex. We can only ponder meaning and purpose because we have words that allow us to explore these areas. Because of our capacity for language, we can both plan ahead and reflect back. We can add rational thought to a process that is otherwise dominated by fear and threat.

These three types of connection span our brain's structure, from most primitive to the more developed. The motivation of each type of connection spans a matrix from the motivation of fear to the motivation of aspiration.

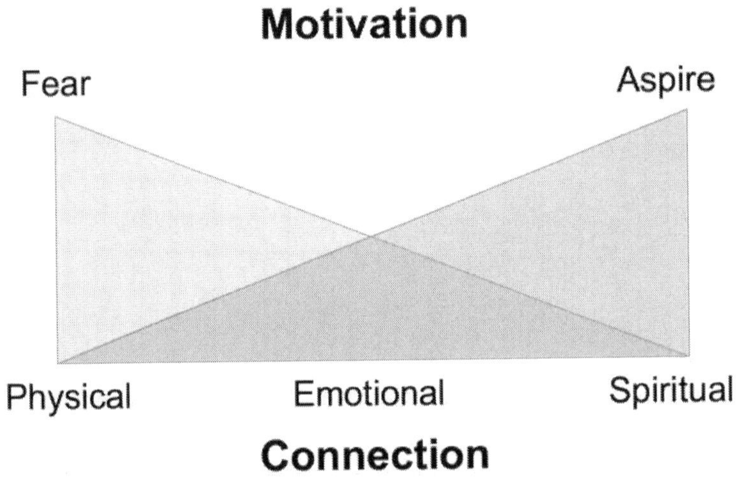

Motivation

Fear Aspire

Physical Emotional Spiritual

Connection

All three areas of connection are necessary and important. Each addresses another layer and aspect of our lives. These areas are needs we all have. When they are missing, we appear more and more needy. People often seek resolution to lacking in any of these areas by looking outside of the marriage relationship.

This is not to say that a marital relationship can or will meet the entirety of anyone's needs in each area. It is, however, the primary place of connection. And that connection is held as safe, because of the commitment that creates the bedrock of the marriage relationship. More than that, if you want to preserve the marital relationship, the points of connection must be addressed. Disconnections need to be addressed and reconnections need to be made.

Let's take a look at your plan to reconnect.

Your Plan To Connect

At this point, you have a clear understanding of the role of connection in the marital relationship. Hopefully, you have spent some time reflecting on the areas where the connection may have been missing or in deficit. If you have not, please spend some time examining the three areas of connection in your own relationship.

Now it is time for you to begin the work of reconnecting. You may be attempting to address areas where you have become disconnected. You may also be attempting to address areas where the connection has always been lacking. In either case, the important thing is to make sure that you have a plan in mind and that you focus on that plan.

There are some "rules" of connecting that are important for you to keep in mind. These are more guidelines than rules, as they are not absolute. But in my experience, these guidelines can be very helpful in your being successful with your attempts to reconnect.

9 Rules For Connecting

1) Move slowly.

If you have been disconnected for some time, you do not want to try to jump back into strong connection. If you attempt to move quickly, you will see resistance from your spouse. He or she will quickly back away, be even more "on guard" and resist all attempts to reconnect.

The more disconnected you are, the more slowly you will need to move. And here is the problem: your fear of further deterioration will try to trick you into pushing for connection. Now that you know that connection is the food of the marriage, you will want to feed the relationship as quickly as possible.

Let me offer an analogy. When a child is starving in a Third

World country, feeding stations have learned that you cannot simply load that child up with food. In fact, too much food will collapse the child's system which is not used to enough sustenance. Too much food pushes the child's body beyond what it can handle, and the child can suddenly go from dying from too little food to dying from too much food. The nutrition must be added slowly and increased slowly.

Remember that it took time for the relationship to become disconnected. It will take time for the relationship to reconnect. Be patient and move slowly. Desperation is your enemy at this point in the process.

Add a little bit at a time and allow it to be digested before you add more. For example, let's assume that the physical connection is missing. "Going for it" and hoping to have sex is way beyond what the relationship can handle. Have you been kissing? Have you been hugging? Have you been cuddly with each other when in bed or sitting on the couch? Have you been holding hands? Have you been touching in passing?

Each of these actions is, in reverse order, the process of moving toward deeper physical connection and intimacy. In other words, if you start at the end of the list, move upward to the point where you are. If you do not touch at all, then start with touching in passing. Where are you on the list below?

- ✓ Touching in passing.
- ✓ Holding hands.
- ✓ Sitting close and cuddling on the couch, then in the bed.
- ✓ Hugging each other for more than just a "grab and release."
- ✓ Kissing for more than a peck on the cheek or lips.
- ✓ Caressing and touching.
- ✓ Sexual touch and intercourse (they are not the same!).

This list gives you something of a roadmap for rebuilding the physical connection. But remember, physical connection is much more primal and may be heavily protected by your spouse.

In terms of emotional connection, remember the acronym "A.R.E."? Are you Accessible, Responsive, and Engaged?

Remember that being accessible is more than just the fact that you are physically present in the house. Or that you are physically present around your spouse. Being accessible means that you are paying attention when your spouse is speaking. You're not watching TV, you're not reading, you're not looking at the paper, you're not looking at your smart phone, or your iPad, Kindle, or any other distraction. When you are accessible, your spouse knows that you are listening to what he or she is saying. You are a part of their conversation, not just being available for it.

Being responsive is when you see your spouse having a difficult time, and you're willing to help your spouse through that process. In other words, you are responding to the emotional state of your spouse and you are aware of the emotional process that is going on in his or her life, and work to respond to it — not to fix the problem, but to be with your spouse while he or she is working through the emotions of the situation.

Being engaged is a bit more problematic if you and your spouse are disconnected on an emotional level. The reason for this is because engagement comes when both of you feel like you're in sync with each other. It is difficult to be in sync with each other if you have been disconnected. But there is another area of this connection, and that is the fact that you have a common history. You have inside stories and jokes between you. You have understandings that have built over the years. You can use these moments, memories, and inside jokes to foster the sense of being in sync with each other. You don't want to force this, but when something comes up that reminds you of someplace that you've been together, for example, you can remind yourselves of that connection.

One of the things that happens when a couple is disengaged and disconnected is that the individuals begin to tell a story in their heads about how little they have in common. This is not a true story, but a fictional account of the path. In fact, it is often brought up to each other. Usually, the one who is thinking about leaving the relationship will remind the other about how "little we have in common." This is a justification for the reason why things are not working out, and why they are an issue.

The truth is, every couple has a great deal in common. You have a history together. You have experiences together. For many, you'll have kids and finances in common. You may not share the same hobby or interest, or perhaps even some of the same long-term plan. But it would be a very boring world if the only people that we hung around with were those that were exactly identical to us. The same is true in a marriage. Marriages become stagnant when the requirement is for both people to see things just alike and do everything together. (That is NOT being a WE, which requires two people with different viewpoints, working together to make it through life. It is not a mind-meld.)

Don't be thrown off by comments made by your spouse that indicate that you have nothing in common. This is just more of the self-justifications that people do when marriages are in a crisis. Don't take it personally and don't try to defend it. Do not enter into a debate to prove your spouse wrong. Your spouse will only work harder to prove him/herself right.

Spiritual connection is at the opposite end from physical affection. By that, I mean that spiritual connection comes from a very different place than physical connection. There are many couples who maintain a successful relationship with very little spiritual connection. They have strong emotional connection and strong physical connection, and that carries them through the missing spiritual connection. But there are few couples that can thrive when they have a spiritual connection but no physical connection and/or no emotional connection.

If you find that spiritual connection has been missing in your relationship, look first to make sure that the emotional connection and the physical connection are well-established before pushing too much into this arena. That doesn't mean you avoid it, but that you don't make spiritual connection your biggest target.

It is likely that you may need to work on exploring your own spiritual life, your own internal growth, before you can share it with your spouse. We will be looking at that in the section on changing yourself.

If you look at your relationship and see that there is a disconnection in the physical area, emotional area, and the spiritual area, let me make a suggestion that you begin your focus on the emotional connection. It is safer, as it stands between the two other levels of connection. On the continuum between fear and aspiration, emotional connection is in the middle. It is not that it is devoid of fear, or devoid of aspiration, but it straddles the two zones. So it will feel less threatening for both you and your spouse. If you decide to focus on the emotional connection, don't ignore the other two, but don't make them your biggest emphasis. Emotional connection is by far the safest place to begin the process of reconnection.

2) Be Calm, Constant, and Consistent.

I seem to love the letter C. I have the 3 C's of saving your marriage, and the 3 C's of connecting. So, these create my $3C's^2$ process. These three C's of connection require serious attention.

The first C is **calm**. You want to work on remaining calm throughout the process of reconnecting. This is crucial. Remember us talking about that very primitive part of the brain that is looking for threat? When you are not calm, you are activating that center in both your spouse's brain and your brain. It will keep your spouse on high alert and keep you keyed up on adrenaline. This will make it very difficult for you to make progress. It's quite the conundrum, isn't it? At a time when you are anxious and fearful about losing a relationship, I am telling you that you need to remain calm. I know it's a tall order. But it is extremely important that you work to remain calm.

The first step in remaining calm is taking care of yourself. There is a physiological reality to fear and stress. The more you can take care of your physiological issues, your biological needs, the calmer you will be. Make sure you are eating healthily, getting exercise, and getting enough sleep. My suggestion is that during this time, you minimize your exposure to sugar and carbohydrates. The fact is, your body is in fight/flight mode. So it is craving quick calories. Unfortunately, the quick calories we often crave are sugar-laden – rich in carbohydrate. While you may be craving them, as they convert in your body, they only add to the adrenaline flowing through your system. This is the antithesis of staying calm.

If you haven't been exercising, now is a good time to begin light exercise. At least take a walk of 20 to 30 minutes once or twice per day. That would be a bare minimum. The reason for this is because the adrenaline flowing through your body has to be processed in some way by your body and activity is one way of processing it. Being active burns off the adrenaline, allowing your body to return to a state of calm.

Similarly, sleep is important to keep your body from overreacting to the adrenaline. Your body needs somewhere between seven and nine hours of sleep; it doesn't need more and it certainly doesn't need less. The less sleep you have, the more adrenaline-laden your body is. The more sleep you get, past what is necessary, the more lethargic your body will become, keeping you from being optimal in your attempts at saving your marriage. This is the time to be working on becoming your healthiest self. In fact, this focus on health will dovetail into the next process of working on yourself, of becoming a better person.

The second C is **constant**. Being constant refers to the fact that you want to be working on this process of reconnecting on a constant level. That does not mean every minute of every day, or even every hour of every day. It does mean that you don't reach out in connection one week and then wait three more weeks to do something else. By constant, I mean that you reach out in connection on a regular basis. If you are very disconnected, a "regular basis" may be every couple of days. If you are still living in the same house, even sharing the same bed, then it may be a couple of times a day that you reach out and make a new and conscientious attempt to reconnect.

The important thing about "constant" is that the level of regularity is not out of desperation, but it is also not neglected. Remember, neglect is likely what got you here in the first place. Few people set out to create a disconnected relationship. Life gets in the way, and we get derailed from a process of building a good marriage. And when we are derailed, the neglect only grows. So being constant is important in this process.

The third C is **consistent**. You want to be consistent with your attempts to reconnect; in other words, you don't want to keep changing tactics, which only leads to confusion on the part of your spouse. Once you have created your plan, stick with it. Don't change tactics just because you read an article, read a book, or saw something that gave you another idea that is *in contradiction* to the plan that you have chosen. There are a myriad of opinions out there. Many don't agree with each other. Some are even opposite of each other. Don't fall into the trap of trying the "next best idea" to save your marriage. Pick your plan and then be consistent with working on the connection through that plan.

Being consistent, though, doesn't mean that you only do one thing over and over and over. It just means that the ways in which you seek connection are all consistent with each other, and that you are consistent with using those techniques. You can fulfill all three areas of connection by using a number of ways that would be consistent with each other. My concern is pulling an idea from one place and then using the opposite idea.

For instance, I'm suggesting that you reach out and work on the connection. Let's assume that you begin to work your plan and that you are working to reconnect. Then you read somewhere that the best thing you can do is to make yourself jealous. So, you decide to stop communicating. You decide to stop all connection. You stop calling, you stop texting, you stop being available, you stop hugging, or any other technique that you've created for connecting. You decide that you're willing to wait for your spouse to reach out toward you. Now that is an approach, one that you will find in some programs. But it is inconsistent with an approach of trying to reconnect. It is also an approach that I have rarely seen be successful.

If you find another idea on how to connect — and it is in agreement with the plan you are already making — then add it in. It is like when you are exercising and find another effective exercise to either augment or replace what you are doing. It is still moving you toward the goal you have. Here, the goal is to connect in a consistent manner.

As you work to reconnect, remember the 3C's of connection: Be Calm, Be Constant, Be Consistent.

3) Do not use connection for your own reassurance.

This morning, I was looking through my emails, as I do every morning. I find them to have very consistent themes that have remained consistent in the last decade of me being online. People write to me, telling me that they want to save their marriage, but they're not sure if their spouse wants to. They tell me that they don't want to do anything until they know whether or not their spouse wants to save their marriage. I understand the sentiment, but I disagree with it. I firmly believe that you can begin the process of saving your marriage, even if your spouse wants nothing to do with it. There are times when the process will fail. You don't have full control over that, and you have to give up a desire to have control, in order to work a process by yourself.

One of the hallmarks of people who tell me this is that they want reassurance from their spouse before they "take a risk" on saving their marriage. I certainly understand, and it is frightening to be facing a marriage crisis, and more frightening to not know how it can be resolved. So, a common reaction is for people to try to find reassurance that the process is moving forward. They seek it out from their spouse. This is very dangerous to the process.

The issue of reassurance brings us to the reason for not trying to use connection to get reassurance. When you are trying to get reassurance, and there is a crisis, it is very easy for you to become, or appear to become, needy. Neediness is not an attractive trait, especially when the marriage is in crisis.

I often see people try to reach out in connection, especially around physical connection, as a way of getting reassurance for how things are going. They report to me any new details about the reactions to a hug or a kiss or an attempt to hold hands. That tells me that they are using the physical connection as reassurance, or more likely as lack of reassurance of the process. What they want to have happen when they reach out for a hug is for their spouse to grab them, hug them hard, apologize for what has happened, and pledge their undying love. That's the script that people write in their heads. That's rarely the reality of what happens.

So, decide that you will reach out to connect. But decide that you're going to reach out to show your connection — as a way of showing your love. Do not seek reassurance in the connection. This is especially true with physical connection. Let your attempts to connect be an energy flowing from you to your spouse, and not seeking energy from your spouse.

4) Do not "read the tea leaves."

When I was a teenager, I was a fairly decent magician and became friends with lots of other magicians. That led to meeting some very interesting people. One group of people I met were the carnies. These were people who follow the carnivals around the country. I remember one of these people, a dear old Gypsy woman. That's actually how she billed herself. She was the fortuneteller for the carnival. And I'm convinced that she truly believed that she could read fortunes. Her specialty was reading tea leaves. Someone would come into her tent, and the Gypsy would put tea leaves in the bottom of the cup, pour in the hot water, slurp it loudly, swirl it around, and then look at the tea leaves at the bottom. From there, she would weave a long story about what was going to happen in the future for the person who was paying her. There were incredible stories about the woes and the hopes, all from looking at tea leaves.

She was looking for a pattern in the swirls and believed that the pattern foretold the future. We all do the same thing. We try to read the tea leaves. This is especially true when we are not getting clear messages about what's coming our way. For example, when there is a marriage crisis and a spouse is not telling you about his or her intention. When there is anxiety and uncertainty, it is common to try to "read tea leaves."

I have had people who have come to my office to tell me that all is lost, because the spouse was upset with them in the morning. Then they get home in the afternoon and find out that there was nothing in that conversation in the morning that had to do with them or the marriage. At other times, I've had people come in my office and tell me that their spouse called them back, so everything must be okay. They return home, only to find that nothing has changed and their marriage is still in crisis. In other words, if you look at what happened and try to read something into it, you are reading tea leaves. You are creating a fictional story, one that may have nothing to do with reality. Remember, fiction sometimes has elements of reality. The danger is believing that it is entirely reality.

So, my guideline, or rule, is to not read tea leaves. Don't try to foretell what is going to happen based on what you're reading into patterns from your spouse's behavior. Don't take actions or attitudes as positive or negative. Don't fill in missing information as a good sign or a bad sign. Stay consistent with your plan, stay constant with your plan, and be calm, regardless of what you see. There will be lots of bumps, ups and downs, forward movement and backward movement, before the end of the story is told. And you can't foretell it. Neither can I. So don't try.

Don't read the tea leaves.

5) Work to connect on all three levels: Physical, Emotional, and Spiritual.

We have already talked about the three different food groups of connection. Remember, a balanced diet is important. You will want to be working on all three areas. As I previously noted, you want to first be emotionally connected, then working on physical connection, then adding in the spiritual connection. But you still want to be focused on all three areas.

Every couple has a different pattern of how they have connected in the past. There may have been more emphasis on one area than another. This is like the food groups. Some people like carbohydrates, some people like fats, and some people like proteins. But a balanced diet requires eating from all three groups. You may have favorite food groups and favorite ways of connecting, but balance comes when all three areas and groups are attended to. They don't have to be equal, just like a diet may not be equally pulling from different types of nutrients. It is just that all three areas have a need and a place in your connection diet.

Stay focused on all three areas. Make sure that as you're working to restore the connection, you don't overemphasize one level, to the detriment of another level.

6) Connect in ways that your spouse desires(ed).

You may be wondering about how you should connect. Let me give you a hint. *Look at the ways that your spouse has tried to connect with you.* Don't keep your focus on how your spouse is currently trying to connect with you, because your spouse may not be trying anymore. If your spouse is still connecting with you, you will certainly want to attend carefully to how your spouse connects. This will give you hints on how your spouse feels most connected.

But also think back to the past. What were the ways that you and your spouse connected in the past? Some of those ways may be out of reach right now. Still, look for a pattern. What were the general ways that you connected? Did you enjoy trying new things, then talking about it afterwards? Did you set aside time to take a walk and chat?

We all have favorite ways of connecting and types of connections that let us feel more connected. If you are familiar with Gary Chapman's book, *The Five Love Languages*, this idea is very similar. Dr. Chapman asserts that there are five basic ways of showing love. According to Chapman, we each understand love best through one or two of these "languages." On his list of love languages are: quality time, physical touch, gifts, words of encouragement, and acts of service. When spouses speak different "love languages," each can feel out of synch and unloved, even if this is not true.

The same is true with connection. Dr. Chapman is speaking

about how we express love. This is similar, but a bit different than connecting. What is the same is that when we do not express connection or love in ways that a spouse can understand, the spouse can feel unloved or disconnected.

Within each area of connection: physical, emotional, and spiritual — make a list of how you and your spouse have connected. Take some time to think about how you connected in each area in the early stages of your relationship. What made you feel close?

Take a moment to also remind yourself that the place in your mind that is saying "What about me? Why isn't my spouse trying to figure out how to best connect with me?" is not serving you or the process of saving your marriage. If you are working on your marriage by yourself, part of the process is setting aside your own wants, needs, and desires for the time-being. This is the time to focus on what will reconnect you. It is not the time to get trapped in playing the "It's not fair" game in your head. This is a temporary time. When things are back on track, the balance can return.

7) Expect that it will take some time.

Don't allow yourself to become discouraged or frustrated. Stay upbeat. This is a mental game, but an important one. When you allow yourself to become discouraged, you will stop working your plan. You will start playing the "It's not fair" tape in your mind.

Focus on this being a long-term process. In fact, even after your marriage is back on-track, the process continues. While it is much more fun when things are moving in a positive direction, the process of (re)building a marriage is lifelong. Take the long-term view at this point.

Remember that marriages do not get into trouble overnight, and problems are not solved overnight. It takes time to change habits. It takes time to make relational shifts. It takes time to see results.

As I mentioned in the introduction, several years back, I got a rude "wake up call" from my body. I spent six months with a pretty serious illness. My days amounted to dragging my body into work, dragging back home, and loading up on medicines to keep moving. I am a pretty stubborn guy, so I kept going to work, but that was about all I could manage. I felt horrible.

When I was mostly through the illness, I realized something: I had neglected my health and my body. And when you neglect your health and body, it will come back to haunt you, much like neglecting a marriage and relationship. I was eating poorly, out of shape, and overweight. And I was scared. Sound familiar to reactions to a marriage crisis? The doctor told my wife I was 85% likely to be totally disabled. And eventually, according to the information I found on the internet, this illness would kill me. Except it didn't. I was very fortunate.

But it woke me up!

I had to take a long reassessment and look at what I was doing in my life and how I was treating my health and body. And I realized I needed to do things differently. I had a lifelong desire to learn to SCUBA dive, and my wife gave me lessons as a gift. I remember the first day of class, and the swimming test. I passed. It was not pretty, but I passed. I pulled myself out of the pool, out of gas and out of breath, looked up at the instructor and said, "I got the message." That started a process of taking better care of myself.

I started eating better and exercising. And slowly, I got into better shape. I had more energy. I was gaining ground. There were plenty of times that I just wanted to be better — in better shape and in a better place. But it took time.

And here is the thing I want you to remember: it took time for my body (and your marriage) to fall apart. It happened without my (and probably your) noticing it. The decline was slow and steady. And I kept making excuses (did you?) about things. "Too tired," "Too busy," "Will do it later," etc. I look back on pictures of me before I got sick, and I am appalled on how I had let myself get into such poor shape.

It took time to decline and it took time to improve. In fact, it has now been a decade since that health crisis, and I continue to improve my health. Even after steady efforts, I find new areas upon which to improve. I have discovered that health is a process. It can always be improved. I can always learn more about taking care of myself.

And the same is true with your marriage. It is a long-term project, and the crisis can be just the impetus to get you moving toward something great. Just accept that it will take some time to get there. Be patient.

8) Formulate your plan.

Let me suggest that you not "wing it." Sit down and think about how you are going to approach this reconnection. This is a crucial part of your efforts to save your marriage. Do not take it lightly. Spend some time thinking about what actions you will take, specifically. It is too easy to just say, "Okay, I will reconnect on the three levels, and I will make sure I do it consistently." That is step one. Step two is to be specific and clear on your plan. Don't leave it in your head, either. Write. It. Down. I mean it! Take the time to write it down. This is the only way to truly commit to it, and it gives you something to remind you of what you are doing. Our minds tend to play tricks on us. We rewrite our intentions over time. And eventually, we find ourselves derailed. If you need help on creating that plan, you can grab my Save The Marriage System at www.SaveTheMarriage.com.

Step One, decide you will make a plan. Step Two, make a plan. Then Step Three, stick to your plan.

9) Refuse to be pulled into anger/resentment/ hurt/frustration (your own or your spouse's).

Two destructive emotions in any marriage are anger and resentment. It is important to understand these two emotions and how to deal with them.

Anger is a secondary emotion. This is a very important point to understand. Anger is not really the primary emotion. It is an outward reaction to another emotion. The primary emotion is hurt. In fact, anger is always a secondary emotion to hurt, threat, or fear.

This is important to understand, because when you react to the anger, you are missing the underlying feeling. This is true whether it is your anger or your spouse's anger. Respond to the anger, and you'll add fuel to the fire. Respond to the hurt, and you will suppress the fire. You will see the anger subside, but only when the underlying hurt, threat, or fear, is addressed.

Resentment is simply anger that has not been processed, not been released, and is therefore continuing to circulate in the emotional system. It points to the fact that the underlying issues of hurt or threat have not been resolved. It also points to the fact that the anger created by those two emotions has not been released. This is incredibly destructive in a relationship.

Anger is an interesting emotion. Since it is a secondary emotion, you can't address it directly. But when one person is angry, it generally creates anger in the other party. It is rare that we do a good job of addressing another person's anger without getting angry ourselves. Unfortunately, anger begets anger, unless you are very careful. In essence, one person's anger, caused by an underlying hurt, triggers hurt in the other person, which comes out as anger. The cycle can continue indefinitely. It creates hurt that is not addressed and is allowed to grow.

Anger is a dangerous contagion. It will infect you, if you are not careful. Don't let your spouse's anger, resentment, or frustration infect you. One way to do this is to understand the nature of anger. Now that you know the anger is really a secondary emotion to hurt, you know that your spouse is really hurt when he or she is responding with anger. That is an important fact. Now, instead of responding to anger with anger, you can respond to anger by trying to address the underlying hurt. By doing this, you get to the root cause of the anger and clear out the infected hurt. You clean the wound, so it doesn't become inflamed and angry.

Recognize that your own feelings of frustration and anger, just like those of your spouse, are rooted in hurt. Also recognize that at this time, your hurt may not be addressed. In fact, if you are having a crisis in your relationship, and you are working to save your marriage, it is highly likely that your spouse will not be addressing your hurt. So, try to avoid allowing for hurt to turn to anger. Accept that it is hurt and decide not to allow the infection to grow within you.

Unfortunately, anger is a distancing emotion. It repels us. Hurt, on the other hand, can be an intimacy-building emotion. When somebody is hurt, we usually want to address their pain. When somebody is angry, we usually want to move away from that person. It will take your conscious effort to look at your spouse's anger as an underlying hurt. Work to do that, so that you can address the underlying hurt. Doing so will benefit your spouse, your relationship, and you. For most people, it takes a bit of practice to stop reacting to the anger and start looking for the hurt. We have been trained to respond to anger mostly with anger. Don't continue to fall into that trap.

CHAPTER 9
C-HANGE YOURSELF

Step number one was connecting. Step number two is to change yourself. This is not a separate step, but one that needs to happen simultaneously with working to reconnect. In fact, for some people, the process has to be working to change yourself before your spouse will be willing to accept any of your attempts at reconnecting.

Let me say at the outset that I do not know you. I do not know who you are, how you act, what you believe, or where you may be stuck. But I do know this: we all have places where we can grow and change and improve ourselves. So when I say that you need to change yourself, it is not personal. It is a statement of being human. We all have places where we can be better, or different, than we are. We all have places where we have become stuck. We all have places where we have stopped growing and are only growing stagnant.

We all have needs to change and grow. Stagnation is the enemy of becoming who we need to become. This is not about a deficit in you or criticism of who you are. It is not an attack on your personality, nor any belief on my part that you have created the problems in the marriage. It is, however, an assertion that in life, we all have places where we can become more aligned with our true self.

The reason that changing yourself is so important to saving a marriage is because part of what keeps a marriage stuck is the stagnation of the individuals in the marriage. People get into bad habits. People stop growing. When that happens, we stagnate in the relationship, too. We get in our own way, tripping ourselves up. So we need to change and grow in order to be more capable of saving our marriage and of being the spouse we want to be.

As I noted earlier, one of my favorite quotes is by Ray Kroc, "You are either green and growing or ripe and rotting." For many of us, we have places and areas where we are growing, and lots of places where we are rotting. The rotting is caused by stagnation. Stagnation is what happens when we lose touch with our dreams, stop taking action, and get lost in the day-to-day activities that fill our hours.

In her book, *MindSet*, Carol Dweck notes that there are two mindsets. The first is a **growth mindset**, and the second is a **fixed mindset**. According to Dweck, we all have both. It just depends on the area of life you are looking at. You can have a growth mindset in one area of life and a fixed mindset in another area of life.

A fixed mindset is one that assumes that you cannot grow and change. The fixed mindset is the belief that you are where you are, and you're stuck there. "You can't teach an old dog new tricks" is a fixed mindset. It assumes that at some point in life, you no longer learn new skills. That timeframe can be any point in life. For example, when we tell children that they are "good in math," or they are "a natural athlete," we have assigned a fixed mindset to them. A fixed mindset is not necessarily seeing a negative attribute to somebody, as much as assuming that there is no room for growth or skills acquirement — no learning is necessary or possible.

Whenever we assume that somebody is naturally good or not good at something, we are in the middle of a fixed mindset. If I tell myself that I am just not good at relationships, and that I just can't learn to understand my spouse's emotions, I have assigned myself a fixed mindset. I can do the same with my spouse. And my spouse can do the same with me. In other words, we can assign a fixed mindset to ourselves or to somebody else. But the fact is, we can learn skills and abilities at any point in life, which brings us to the growth mindset.

A growth mindset is the mindset that assumes I can grow and learn new skills at any point. And in fact, this is reality. When I was a child, I was standing at a magic shop at the beach, captivated by a magic trick. The magician who was selling the trick promised me that it was an easy trick, "almost self-working." So, I tossed my five dollars on the counter, grabbed the trick, and headed to the car. We were close to the end of our vacation, and so I set it aside for the trip home.

A couple of days later, after we had left the beach and any opportunity of getting instructions from the magician, I opened the package and discovered that the trick was not so "self-working" as the magician had led me to believe. It required a certain sleight-of-hand. My little hands had never done the movement that it required. I tried it a couple times and could not get it to work. After about ten minutes, I was frustrated with the trick, and frustrated with the magician who sold it to me.

I had been taken advantage of! I pouted for a bit, but the trip home was long. As my boredom grew, I decided to give the trick another try. This time, fueled by my frustration, I decided that I was going to figure out how to do it. After all, that magician had done it, and I decided I could, too. I worked and worked at it. My fingertips were fairly sore after about an hour and a half of giving it a try. And the trick still looked bad. But I continued to try. Then, suddenly, I had it down. My fingers knew what to do. I had figured out how to do that one sleight-of-hand move. From then on, as I tried new trick after new trick, I knew that it was a matter of effort, practice, and figuring out how to do the sleight-of-hand required. From then on, I knew it was not a matter of me being unable to do it, as much as me starting out unable to do it, until the moment I learned it.

Life is constantly throwing us new challenges. If we assume that we cannot grow, cannot learn new traits, we get stuck. When we get stuck, we grow stagnant. And, we miss the fact that almost everything in life that we need to do is a matter of acquiring skills, learning a new mindset, or picking up a new perspective.

A growth mindset is not an assumption that you can be the best in anything you set your mind to. There are some limits we all live within. While I am 6'4" tall, I cannot wish or make myself taller so that I can be an NBA player. But if I want to be better at basketball, it is a matter of practice. Growth is not about an absolute result as much as it is about the process of improvement.

For example, as a writer, I cannot make myself a "best-selling author." That comes as a result of, well, sales. However, I can work on my writing and I can learn to publicize my book better. I can make sure I contact people who can help. I can certainly improve the possibility that my writing will be seen by many people. I can follow a process of improvement in writing and distributing the book. I cannot guarantee the result of the book being a best seller.

I say this because many people use the thought process of "I can't just be anything I want to be, so this growth mindset doesn't work." If you haven't noticed, built into that argument is a fixed mindset. I would simply argue that with attention and practice, it is always possible to improve in an area of your choosing.

When working to save your marriage, it is important to adopt a growth mindset around relationships and personal development. In the last section, we examined the idea of connection and examined some skills of connection. We looked at a number of guidelines for connecting. If you found yourself saying, "I can do that. I see places to improve," you adopted a growth mindset. You can see that new ideas and thinking give you opportunities of working on the connection in a different way.

It is time to apply that same thought process to yourself. Do you view yourself as a "work in progress," or do you see yourself as stuck or finished? Do you see yourself as having more places to grow and develop, or have you reached a point where you feel that you have either arrived or have landed?

If you want to save your marriage, you will want to shift to a place where you see yourself as becoming. You will want to shift to a growth mindset, one that allows you to develop yourself and the relationship.

From Stagnation to Change

Stagnation comes from a focus on limitations. As life progresses, we often find ourselves aware of the many things that can no longer happen, the path not taken, the places that we cannot go because of the decisions we made earlier. These are limitations we create — limitations we create in our mind that are not reflected in reality. Because with every limitation, we've also created opportunities. Unfortunately, our human mind tends to go toward the limitations rather than the opportunities.

We have a choice to move to conscious living. This is an awareness that life is not a "dress rehearsal." It's an awareness that life is going on around us, even when we are waiting for life to begin. When we are focused on conscious living, we are aware of the fact that time is passing, and we can either embrace the potential, or be caught in the limitations. Life is lived moment by moment, and when we fail to see this, we lose our life to the pain of the past and to the angst of the future. It's important to shift to this "conscious living," in the process of saving your marriage.

A central issue is the decision to take personal responsibility for your life. In fact, I would encourage you to take 100% responsibility for your life. But before you think I am blaming you, please be clear about what I mean.

In the midst of a marital relationship, you cannot take full responsibility for everything that happens or has happened in the relationship. But that does not mean you cannot take responsibility for your life. In fact, stagnation is one way that we deny our own responsibility for living. We look to the limitations, the dead ends, the closed doors, and the "circumstances of life" that keep us from doing what we want to do. More often than not, these are excuses we tell ourselves. They are ways that we avoid responsibility and ways we let ourselves off the hook when things don't go the way we want them to.

This is human nature, but not particularly helpful in the process of saving a marriage. Instead, what I suggest is that you adopt a more radical approach of deciding that you are taking full responsibility for your life. There will be circumstances with which you will have to deal. That does not change responsibility.

We sometimes confuse responsibility and blame in our culture. Blame is all about fault — finding who caused something, who can be blamed for something, who is at fault. Blame is a way of avoiding responsibility.

Responsibility is deciding to deal with whatever comes your way, to make the best of the situation, and to move ahead, in spite of limitations. We get stuck by blame, and we are freed through responsibility.

If I find myself in a burning house, I can decide to do everything I can to get myself out of the house and to make sure that everyone else is safe. That is responsibility. If I stand around trying to figure out who caused the fire, that is blame. Blame keeps me stuck. Taking responsibility to do what I can delivers me safely out of harm's way.

Consider for a moment the process of saving your marriage. It is all too easy to start looking for blame. "Who caused the problem?"

"Where did our difficulties begin?" "Who needs to make a change?" These questions lead us into blame.

"What can I do to change the marriage?" "What can I do to improve myself?" These questions lead to responsibility — which leads to the potential for change.

One of my major concerns with marital therapy is this very point. Many times, the therapy process becomes a process of establishing blame (although the process is more subtle and does not call it blame). There is often a pattern of finger pointing and theorizing about what has happened. Many times, it is like an archeology dig. We go digging up the past — old fights, old hurts, and old difficulties. Then we try to slowly piece together "What went wrong." As far as I can tell, no archeological digging has ever located a living being. Instead, it only finds facts about what happened in the past.

Let me invite you to turn your attention to what could be. What could become of the relationship? How could the relationship grow? How might your relationship become a marriage that you are proud of, that other people point to as a model?

Those questions shift us to potential. From there, creativity is possible. You can imagine what you want the relationship to become. And in that process, you can take responsibility for what you can do to move the relationship forward to a new point.

Taking Action

When you decide to take responsibility for doing what you can to save your marriage, you also have decided to take action.

What often stops us from taking action is fear. In fact, you may notice a common theme throughout this material. Fear is a huge trigger. Fear is what often keeps us from connecting. Fear is what often keeps us from confronting problems in relationships. Fear is what lurks behind anger (fear and hurt are closely connected). Fear is what keeps people from taking responsibility. Fear is what keeps people from changing.

The bad news is that there is no antidote to fear. As we have explored elsewhere, fear is woven into our biology. Your body and your brain are created to react to threats, real or perceived. Your human response to these threats is fear. It affects your brain, body, and mind. And it is inescapable.

But before you give up, there is another option. You cannot escape fear, but you can choose to act in spite of it. As humans, we spend an inordinate amount of time and energy avoiding the feeling of fear. If something makes us fearful, we work to avoid it from happening again. When we do this, the initial trigger for fear grows in power over us.

When my son was younger and a Cub Scout, I was one of the leaders of his scout den. One evening, the boys were talking and discussing someone being brave. I asked the boys to tell me their definition of bravery. To a child, they agreed that bravery was when you do not have any fear. They noted that when people are acting bravely, they are not feeling any fear, so they can act bravely.

I suggested they rethink their definition. I told them, "For me, it is not brave to do something when you have no fear. That is just the act of doing something. Bravery is when you feel fear, and then choose to do the thing that makes you afraid."

Over time, I came to realize that the boys' mistake is a common mistake for people. They came to believe that if they have fear, they should not do something. In reality, fear should only be a small factor in choosing to act. Bravery is when something makes you fearful, but knowing it is the right thing to do, you choose to do it anyway, not because of a lack of fear, but in spite of fear.

Courage is what I am suggesting. Be courageous in your decision to take action. Don't allow yourself to be derailed from the process by your own feelings of fear. They will be there. Just don't allow the feelings of fear to dictate your response.

Your Plan To Change

Marriage crises are a combination of a relational crisis and a personal crisis. The relational crisis exists between the spouses. A necessary level of connection has failed. As that connection drops below the sustaining level, it begins to show other points of weakness. One that consistently emerges is a need for personal growth.

When "Jarod" and "Sue" came to my office, their marriage crisis was well under way. Jarod spent long hours at the office and Sue was working her job and then coming home to take primary responsibility for raising their two teenaged children. In other words, the marital relationship was getting neglected. While both were fully committed to raising their children to be healthy and successful, they had defocused away from their relationship together.

The disconnection was deep and the hurt was great. Neither felt particularly supported by the other, and both were more than willing to point to the shortcomings of the other. Sue claimed that Jarod was "married to his work." She was convinced that home was simply a convenient place for Jarod to sleep, eat, and get ready for work. Work, she said, was where he spent himself. The family just got the leftovers.

Jarod was no less convinced of Sue's shortcomings. He noted that she seemed to love going to HER job, too, and felt it unfair for her to criticize the fact that he enjoyed his work. Jarod also noted that Sue no longer took care of herself, dressed in "sack-y clothes," and had no hobbies or interests. Sue countered that not only did Jarod stay at the office for 12 hour days, but that he also found the time to take four-hour bike rides when he was not at work.

And for the next couple of sessions, neither Jarod nor Sue was willing to examine their relationship. They spent the time highlighting the each other's "shortcomings" as individuals. No matter how insistent I was to return us to the relationship, both were more than capable of pulling the conversation back to the personal — at least the other person's "personal!"

This is typical of a marriage crisis. The focus is on the problems of the other person. The relationship itself, the marital relationship that is in crisis, takes a backseat to the blame game. What ends up missing from the conversation is a discussion about the connection, and the personal responsibility of the two people in that connection.

This is why it is important to attend to both the relationship (connection) and the individual (changing yourself). Both are necessary to reestablish a successful relationship.

Which brings us to the task of working to change yourself. While you are working to connect, you also want to keep a focus on changing yourself. To remind you, this is not a personal attack, or a statement of something being fundamentally wrong with you. It is simply a statement of the fact that we all have places that need to grow, and we all have places where we have grown stagnant.

My hope is that at this point, you've become at least a little bit excited about the possibilities that lie in front of you, both in the relationship and in your own personal growth. So we want to jump into the process of changing yourself, of growing and developing as an individual.

9 Rules for Changing Yourself

Just like in the section on connecting, I want to provide for you some rules on changing yourself. Like the section on connecting, these are more guidelines than rules. But I hope that you will attend to them and treat them as very important, as you work to change yourself.

1) Create a vision of what you want to become.

I want you to spend some time thinking about the new person you want to be. Create a mental picture, and even a written description of what you will be like. This is an important step. Any process of change involves an assessment of the situation, and an understanding of what you want to move toward. If you want to take a trip, you want to have a destination in mind. That allows you to create a map, which allows you to know, step-by-step, what needs to happen in order for you to arrive at your destination. This is no different when the destination is "a new self." Without a realization of what you want to move toward, you will make little progress.

Your first description does not have to be complete. It's the starting point, the beginning of an exploration. Think of this effort as more of a journey of self-discovery, with several points along the path. Each new point or destination moves you to an understanding, a new perspective, which in turn gives you a broader understanding of your next destination. You will always be a work in progress. But you start at the point where you can see the next place you want to be.

For many people, daily life pulls us away from the important factors of life. Our day-to-day existence keeps us from examining the deeper, more important destinations of life. For example, usually, at some point in life, we lose track of moving toward what brings us a sense of meaning and purpose in life. I want you to get back to the place of considering what brings meaning and purpose into your life. But I also want you to think about the areas of life that represent places that you may have outgrown.

We all have patterns of behavior and thought that are no longer serving us, which we may have outgrown. But we still hang on to these patterns. Sometimes, we hang onto the patterns because it's more convenient and keeps us from having to make a change. Sometimes, we hang onto the patterns because it keeps us from having to take full responsibility for our lives. Either way, it keeps us stuck. This is a good opportunity to move beyond those patterns.

Exercise:

Take a bit of time to sit down and do this exercise: think about your ideal life. What would it be like? I want you to spend half an hour each day for the next three days, describing your ideal life. What would you be doing? How would you be interacting with people? Where would you be? Where would you live? Start with the moment that you wake up. What are your surroundings like? What do you do to start your day? Continue this process through your entire day. Describe what your job is like. Describe the people who surround you. Note how you would spend your time.

After you have completed this exercise over the next three days, make a list of all of the changes that have to happen in order for you to move from where you are to how you describe your ideal day. Be specific about this. What are the specific things that have to happen in order for you to shift from your current location to your new life? This will give you a list of items and areas that need to change in order for you to grow into your new place of being. Don't skip this step!

When you get to that place where you say, "My ideal life is not possible," pretend that it is and keep making your list of the changes that would need to happen. Remember, we are not writing what WILL happen, but what you would like your life to be. It is not a prognosis but a description.

Set aside your description of your ideal life and the list of the necessary changes.

2) Accept that we all have places of growth.

When you are working to change yourself, it's easy to play mind games with yourself. You can question why you have to make the changes, and why your spouse is not changing. You can decide that you like who you are, and you don't want to work at the changes. But what I'm asking you to do is acknowledge that there are areas in which we all can grow. There are places that we all have to grow into, and places that we need to leave behind. This is just human nature. It means nothing about you, or any deficits that you might imagine. It is just the reality of the fact that we all have places of growth. So decide to make a change; don't do it with an understanding that there's something wrong with you, but that there's more inside of you that could be right. There are better places for you to grow into, where you can develop and become more than you are.

Take this on as an experiment. It is a period of discovery and of realizing all of the places that you might want and need to grow.

One of the joys of my life is the fact that each week, I get to spend an hour on the phone with my team of Relationship Coaches. I've handpicked this group of coaches to be on my team because of their excellence and because of their capacity in helping others to grow. So each week, we have a conference call together.

What that means is that once a week, I am confronted with the areas into which I need to grow. I'm challenged to find new ways of being, interacting, and doing. I treasure these times, because I see it as an experiment in pushing me to become more than I am. And I invite you to adopt the same level of excitement about the possibility of change. Many times, in the midst of a marriage crisis, we find ourselves weighed down with all of the problems going on. People feel that there is so much to work on, and so much that needs to be changed, and so many things that need to be fixed, that you might miss the fact that life is handing out an opportunity for growth. We simply have to step into a new space of experimenting, so that we become more than we have been and we find a new relationship.

3) Notice the consistent feedback you receive from the world.

If you want a shortcut into the areas that need attention and growth, simply listen to the feedback around you. Start with your spouse. Think about the different criticisms and frustrations your spouse may have expressed about you. Are there some pieces that are consistent over time? Are there some areas that are repeatedly being pointed out to you? Make a list of these items, specifically. Take some time to create this list.

I understand that this is not a fun exercise. Nobody likes criticism. And typically, when we hear criticism, we justify and defend ourselves — and we miss the opportunity we have to grow from criticism.

Annette, one of my coaches, some time ago said that she had come to see criticism as "free coaching." Whenever she found herself being criticized, she worked to try to hear it as points of potential learning. Notice that I said "potential." Not every criticism that comes your way is factual or reflective of you. Sometimes, it has more to do with the other person. But, it is useful to hold the possibility in your mind that the criticism is something that could be constructive if one pays attention. In other words, it may be an area of growth.

Make your list of the consistent criticisms you have received from your spouse and note the themes that might be present in the criticisms. Look for an underlying and consistent theme throughout the criticisms. If you find it, you may have located a new area of growth for yourself. Then, consider these questions: Has the same theme emerged elsewhere in your life? Has it come out at work? Has it come out with friends?

The reason we start with your spouse is because there is no more intimate connection we have with anyone. A spouse usually gives good feedback, because a spouse sees you in many situations. More than that, often, friends withhold judgment. They might be hesitant to tell you when your sense of humor is too biting, or when your listening skills are not up to par, or when you no longer are attending to important things in your own life. But a spouse might tell you all of these things, and many more. So, start with your spouse, and then expand to see if there is any consistency to the theme.

This requires one very important factor from you: self-honesty. Nobody is looking at your list. Nobody is criticizing whether the list is factual or not. Nobody is judging whether you decide to take action or decide not to. Self-development is your own project, and only yours. So you have to be honest with yourself, and look at yourself in the mirror, to decide if what you are hearing, whether you like it or not, may be good feedback.

At this point, you should have a description of your ideal life, and a list of the things that stand between where you are now and that ideal life. You should also have a list of behaviors and thought patterns that you want to change. These are the foundations of your plan for growth and change.

4) Track your changes and your efforts.

Now that you have your list, it's time to begin your growth process and start changing. For the items on your list, begin to make a sub-list of the actions you want to take, the changes you want to make. If you have limiting beliefs that you have stumbled upon, go back to the section on limiting beliefs and work to eliminate them. Don't let your limiting beliefs get in your way of change.

The list of the changes you want to see needs to be specific and actionable. We are creating goals. Without goals, you won't be able to make much progress on the changes you want in your life.

One way of assessing your goals is to use the acronym SMART. Every goal should contain these five elements.

S-pecific. Every goal should be very specific in what it is trying to accomplish. The goal has to be clear and unambiguous. One way of assessing this is to see whether the goal contains the 5 W's:

What – what do I want to accomplish?

Why – why do I want to accomplish this goal? What are the reasons, purposes, and benefits?

Who – who is involved? Primarily, this should be answered by your own involvement.

Where – where is the location that this happens? Does the change need to happen at home? At work? Only with your spouse? With your children? With friends?

Which – which requirements need to be met and what constraints will keep you from having good success?

M-easurable. You must have clear criteria on how to measure your goal. How will you know if you are accomplishing your goal? Sometimes, it will take you a bit of effort to come up with how to measure a goal. But if you cannot measure it, you will not know if you are making progress.

A-ttainable. The goal has to be something that you can accomplish, one that is realistic and attainable. If the goal is too extreme, you will be unable to accomplish it, and you will become frustrated with the process. Lofty goals are fine. Unattainable goals are a waste of time and effort.

R-elevant. Does your goal move you toward your overall goal? Does it move you toward growth and development? Does it move you toward more connection with your spouse? Does it address issues that you have identified in the previous exercises?

T-ime bound. Is your goal one for which you can create a time-frame? Can you give it a target date? Any time frame is fine, but there has to be a time-frame. It may only take you a short amount of time to complete your goal, or it may be a longer-term goal. Either is fine, but there has to be a time-frame that you can assigned to it.

Using this assessment, look through the goals that you have chosen. Do they meet with the criteria? If so, you are ready to begin acting on each specific goal. Be sure and track your efforts on these goals.

If the goals do not match the SMART criteria, rewrite and edit the goals until they do. Remember, the only way to attain a goal is to make sure you understand that goal and understand how you will get to that goal.

5) Recognize that change takes time.

This process is like learning anything new. You are unlikely to be 100% successful at the beginning. Many things that you will try will make you feel awkward. That is the nature of learning new skills and changing habits. This is true at the beginning of learning any skill that you want to accomplish. At first, it will feel foreign and unnatural. But over time, it feels more and more natural, until it becomes a part of you — a habit.

In the last few years, I have had the pleasure of teaching both of my children how to drive. I was reminded that learning to drive is a complex task, requiring multiple skills. When we do it every day, we forget all of the pieces that are involved in the process of driving — until you are trying to describe it to somebody. Then, you realize how complex the process is. You realize how difficult it is to tell someone how to do it. The tasks of coordinating the hand on the steering wheel, the feet on the pedals, and the eyes scanning the road, all while attending to what's happening in the vehicle is a very complex process. In fact, I have read studies that describe it as probably the most complex thing we do on a day-to-day basis. But once we learned how to drive, we promptly forgot how complex it is.

My point is that the same process was true with all of us when we started to drive. Most people felt awkward, and it probably felt to many people as if it were going to be an impossible task. The only reason that most people would continue working at it is because of the freedom driving can give. So, the possibilities of freedom outweighed the difficulties of learning a new skill. It makes us push through the frustrations and awkwardness of the new situation, as a way of getting to a goal.

The same is true for your list. You will find it awkward in the beginning, because it's a new behavior, which is just a new habit. This is true, whether it is a thought habit or a physical habit you are trying to start or change.

This is the reason for writing down your ideal life in the first step. The words remind you of what you want to move toward. It reminds you of what you want to become. It can be your motivation when you're frustrated at the habits that are taking a while to accomplish.

6) Don't try to prove you have changed. Be the change. Live it out.

Whenever we make a change, our tendency is to want to point it out and make sure that everybody notices it. This tendency is partly because we are proud of our changes, and partly because we want to show people that we have moved beyond what we were. You have decided on some changes, because you know that they are important to both you and your spouse. This pressure only increases most people's desire to point out the change. Resist this temptation.

Your spouse is likely to be suspicious of the changes in your life. If you tell your spouse about the changes that you are doing, first, he or she will become suspicious about your motivation. The motivation will be seen as manipulation or as attempts to fool your spouse. Second, your spouse will look for places where you fall short. And you will. That's the nature of learning. You don't want to set yourself up to have your spouse judging how your changing is going. Change is difficult enough without the external pressure to change perfectly.

Instead of telling anybody about your change, be the change. Live it out. Live it out consistently, on a day-to-day basis, regardless of what comes your way. Again, there will be times when you fail. When you fail, simply get started again. Assess what happened — what "pulled you off of your game?" Use this assessment as a learning tool. It is not defeat or failure. It is simply teaching you one more layer to the necessary change.

Often, people get angry with themselves, which is expressed in upset toward people around them, when they don't get the change right. Don't let this happen. Simply assume that every time you don't quite get it right, you're a step closer to getting it right. You learn something new about the process, and about yourself. You can begin to integrate that progress into your goals. This is why you want to track your changes. You want to write down the places where change is difficult, and also places where change was successful.

Accept the places where change is tough. Learn from your mistakes. And celebrate your successes. Remind yourself that you are still in the process of becoming. Remember that growth mindset? It says that we can all grow and improve. But part of the improvement process is that we won't do it perfectly; we will, however, keep on trying until we're successful.

7) Deal with your negative beliefs.

At this point, you will begin to see more negative beliefs in your life. When we start working on changing and growing, we begin to see other areas of limitation. We find other areas where we have limited ourselves by our beliefs. These negative beliefs are our limiting beliefs. It is important to continue to return to the process of ending your negative beliefs. Remember the four C's of ending limiting beliefs. They apply here.

C–onscious. Become clear about the particular limiting belief. Focus on noticing it, so that you are aware of it. Become aware of how it operates in your life. The limiting belief has to be made conscious before anything else can happen.

C–hallenge. Look for things that challenge your limiting belief. Look for proof that your limiting belief is wrong. Find ways to disprove the limiting belief. There is always an abundance of proof that a limiting belief is false. Be open to that fact. Seek out the evidence.

C–hange. Restate your belief in the positive. This changes your perspective. For example, if your limiting belief is that "I can never change," look for times when you have changed. That challenges your belief that you can't change. And there are plenty of opportunities in your life where you will see that you have changed, disproving your core belief. So, state your belief in the affirmative, for example: "I can change."

C–onfirm. Work to find confirmation of your new beliefs by continuing to find evidence that proves your new belief. Look for places where you have changed, for example. When you have been unable to make a change, simply see that you have not yet changed there, but you are capable of it.

8) Solicit help.

Changing yourself can be a challenge; however, people can help you with this. Since you are, at this point, trying to make changes that will improve your relationship, don't seek help from your spouse. Find it from elsewhere. Find a friend, a therapist, a coach, or a mentor, who is capable of listening to you and helping you make the changes you want to make. They should be there to support you, challenge you, and help you stay on track. Accountability is a great thing to have at this point.

Your help should be somewhat objective. A close friend may not do it. Your close friend may let you off the hook and even feed the "blame game" we all like to play. So if you choose a friend (versus professional help), choose carefully. Find someone that will push you and keep you on-track.

9) Be patient with yourself, but insistent on changing.

This is crucial. Change is tough. It is tough for everybody. It's even tougher when you're in the midst of a crisis. And if you feel that there is a short timeframe, a short amount of time in which you have to turn things around, you've only added to your own pressure. Make a choice to be patient with yourself. Change takes time and effort. So be patient with the process, but be insistent that you will be changing. Remind yourself, even when you're tired of the effort, that this is for something good. Remind yourself that change can be fun. Take it on as a challenge. Decide that this is not a punishment, but somewhere that you need to move toward. Embrace it for the potential that it is bringing your way.

Be patient, but insistent on changing.

Showing Up & Saving Your Marriage

How often do we just go through the motions? Do you know what I mean? We sit in front of the computer (or tablet or phone or TV), lost in the media. We check our email, check our texts, follow the hyperlinks, change the station, toss back some chips. . . and suddenly, hours have passed. In other words, while our body is there, we have yet to show up to our own lives!

Let me propose an alternative to this: Show UP! This means to fully be ourselves, to be present, to really bring our greatness to the world.

Now, before that word, "greatness," throws you off, let's talk. I truly believe we all have greatness within us. That doesn't mean we are always showing the world our greatness. Only that it is really in there. (Some of us cover it up very well!)

Your greatness is what others love in you. It is what your spouse came to love within you. And that is the problem. When marriages get into trouble, it is usually true that one or both people have quit showing up.

Oh, sure, you may both be in the same room. But that is not the same as showing up. Showing up is about being present, of showing yourself — your inner world, and of focusing on the other person — including their inner world.

So what would that look like for you? How can you show up? How can you show up MORE? (And we can ALWAYS show up more!)

When your spouse is talking, do you focus on your spouse? Do you listen, showing your interest?

And if you are not interested, why are you not interested? If you are not interested any longer in what your spouse is sharing, you have disconnected a part of yourself. You have stopped showing up.

Reconnect with that part of yourself and you will reconnect with your spouse. Guaranteed.

If you have an inner voice shouting, "Why can't my spouse SHOW UP?" then demand that voice go away. You have no control over how your spouse is showing up. That voice which is judging others is the part of you that is keeping you from showing up. But you do have control over how YOU show up. So choose to show up.

Marriages are saved, in part, by our connection or reconnection, with our better selves. When we demand of ourselves to show up, to be present, we bring ourselves to the relationship in a new way. And guess what? That new way is much more inviting, much more attractive to yourself, your spouse, and the world.

And guess what? Life is ALWAYS better when we truly SHOW UP!

Showing Up and Fear

Marriage is an incredibly intimate relationship. That intimacy is part of what keeps us from showing up. Isn't it ironic that the person we should be closest to, we keep a distance from?

As humans, we have a few fears. These fears keep us from fully engaging. In fact, there are three primary fears that keep us stuck, both in life and in relationships.

Three Primary Human Fears

Fear #1: "I will not have enough."

This basic fear of not having enough is deeply engrained in each of our brains. And even though we live in a world of plenty, with most of us having more than enough to survive, that fear still creeps in. And when it does, we start chasing after more stuff — more money, bigger houses, more food, more toys, more clothes, etc., etc. You will note that most of our accumulating of stuff has little to do with surviving, but the roots are in there.

This fear keeps us in a scarcity mindset, fearful that we will fall short. Remember, reality and fear rarely share the same spot!

One thing to understand: this fear of not having enough has nothing to do with reality. I have met people with millions of dollars in reserve funds who are still fearful that they would not have enough money to make it. This fear drove them to seek out more and more resources and money. The fear drove them so much that they never enjoyed the success they had built. They only tried to get more and more money.

You see, more and more resources do not eliminate this fear. The fear of not having enough, like most fears, cannot be rationally addressed. The fear of not having enough is wired into our brains from the eons of struggling to survive. Those who feared not having enough were driven to make sure there was enough, allowing survival during the lean times. Those who did not share that fear were likely caught unprepared, leaving their gene pool to history.

Fear #2: "I will not be good enough."

This is a fear of competence. Again, it is deeply held. Being "good enough" is a very subjective point. Good enough for what? As children, it may be "good enough at athletics" or "good enough at academics" or "good enough to be liked and accepted."

The feeling of being good enough is a feeling of competence, and can invade any area of our lives: "Am I good enough to fix this relationship?" "Am I good enough to keep my job?" "Am I a good enough parent?" And, many more.

This one fear, while less primal than having enough, trips us up more than any other when we are trying to Show Up in life. Because if you fear not being good enough, you will either strive to prove you are good enough or you will hide to avoid proving you are not good enough.

When I was a child, I struggled with reading. In fact, I pretty much could not read during the first few years of school, and I attempted to prevent anyone from discovering it. I would avoid having to read whenever possible. Every now and then, I couldn't get around it, and I had to read. That was embarrassing. I couldn't hide that I couldn't read at those points. But I dodged it enough that I skated by without detection for the most part.

Until fourth grade. My fourth grade teacher figured it out, and that's when I went to reading class. My struggles with academics went back before that, all the way back to kindergarten. In fact, years later I found that my kindergarten teacher told my mother that I had great limitations in my aptitude and abilities. I internalized that belief and struggled to feel confident to do schoolwork.

Even after I discovered the key to my own method of reading (thanks to my persistent mother), I continued to struggle with feelings of incompetence. In some ways, I wonder, as I look around my office, surrounded with books, if I still struggle with the feeling of confidence around that issue. But I managed to stick with scholastic work, all the way through a PhD. Several times, that feeling of incompetence would limit me and keep me from really engaging in school work. In fact, I often acted in ways that helped me avoid the feeling of incompetence.

For example, when I was a young teenager, my parents knew a psychologist. The psychologist agreed to give testing to my family to help with learning skills. The testing included a personality assessment and core competency testing. I remember when he had finished running tests, that he asked if I wanted to do a couple more tests. If I did the next test, he told me, I would have an accurate IQ score.

I told him I didn't want to do it. The psychologist told me that he already had an estimate, but a couple more tests would nail it down. So, he asked, why did I not want to take the time to get the accurate score? In a moment of clarity, I told him I didn't want my parents to know my IQ score. Because I knew that if they knew my IQ score, they would know that I had been underperforming.

Notice that there are two pieces within me. One piece knows that I am competent and could do better work. The other part of me comes from a place of fear and was afraid to do anything that would force me to claim my competence. It was easier to hide behind my incompetence than to step out into my competence. So, I didn't always show up at school. I was there practically every day. But I didn't really show up throughout most of my schooling.

Looking back, I see that my years of feeling incompetent limited my engagement in my scholastic work. I achieved a Ph.D., but that doesn't mean I was fully invested in the process. In the end, I did not get everything I could have out of my educational opportunities. I limited myself. That's the nature of fear. It limits us.

What are your stories of limitations? Where are the places that you can look back and see that you played it smaller than you could or should have?

Fear #3: I will not be loved enough.

The fear of not being loved enough is, like the other two primary fears, deeply wired into us. We, as humans, are in desperate need of connection. That need for being loved, feeling connected, creates the deep fear that we will not have enough love.

You may have noticed this fear in the midst of your marriage crisis. While this fear is always in the background, nothing stirs a fear like a perceived threat — someone pulling their love away. That feeling of someone pulling away triggers a cascade of emotions and actions that are rarely constructive or helpful. In fact, they are almost always counterproductive.

A few months ago, I received an email from "Sarah." Sarah was telling me about how her husband, much to her surprise, had announced he was not happy and had decided to separate. He moved into an apartment just days after announcing his unhappiness. At first, he said he would go to counseling, but after a contentious therapy session, he refused to go back.

Sarah described to me her reactions to this. During phone calls, while her husband was trying to discuss some practical issues, Sarah would regularly pull the conversation back to her being hurt and angry. At this point, she would continue on a 10 to 15 minute discussion of how unfair her husband had been, how deeply hurt she felt, and how angry she was that she had not had a chance to work on the relationship.

Let me be clear that these feelings were legitimate and fair. But her 15 minute diatribe did little to build any connection in the relationship. Sarah knew this, and yet the words would continue to flow out of her mouth each time they spoke. Not surprisingly, Sarah's husband was less and less willing to talk on the phone. Sarah saw him as just being meaner and more unfair. Her fear, not Sarah's higher self, was doing the communicating. I noted to Sarah that she and her husband had several opportunities to connect, but instead of working on connection, Sarah's efforts led to further distance. Instead of Sarah "showing up" in those phone conversations, fear showed up. When fear shows up, we usually get more of what we fear and less of what we want.

Notice that these three fears we have are self-centered: I will not have enough, be good enough, be loved enough ("I," "I," "I"). The fears are not that we cannot give enough, cannot do enough, and cannot love enough. It is a fear that not enough will come *toward* us. In fact, the antidote to the fears is when we are able to move outwardly (into the world and toward people), and not when we move toward fear inwardly.

Can I be more generous, do more, and love more? By moving in the opposite direction than our fear is pulling, we starve the fear of energy.

When we act on a fear, that fear is fed and grows stronger. The next time that we have the fear, it has a stronger pull upon us. We are easier targets for that fear. We are less able to pull away from it. Notice that I did not say "unable to pull away from it." Only that it takes even more energy.

And it is important to note that these fears will never be starved to death. They will always be there. The question is only in how strongly the fears will control your life. The fears do not have to be eliminated in order to make sure that your life is not dominated by that fear.

As Sarah worked to pull against her fear, she was more capable of having better conversations with her husband. Fear was encouraging her to attack, but her bravery called her to connect and show up. Ironically, when she looked back on her relationship, Sarah realized that her fear of not being loved enough was already at work earlier in the relationship. At some point, she noted, she had stopped connecting from a loving place, and had begun connecting from a desperation place. As the fear grew, her desperation grew. And the growing fear had little to do with any real changes in her husband's behavior.

That's the nature of any fear. It does not need real facts in order for it to grow. Fear grows just as well by feeding on perceptions, allegations, and irrational thoughts as it does on facts and reality. Perhaps even more so.

The starting point is understanding and naming these fears. Next, accept that you have fears and that is normal. Then, accept that fears are not necessarily based in rationality, as most are irrational. Finally, refuse to allow the fears to dictate your actions.

To Show Up Or Not?

During my formal clinical training, I was engaged in a training process called CPE (Clinical Pastoral Education). In this training, I served as a chaplain at a hospital. This process is a way of learning about yourself, while gaining skills of care and counsel. It is a very challenging program for people, pushing people to be more alive and more open than they were before. And that was certainly my experience.

I remember the first day of CPE. It was a very instructive moment for me. My supervisor was a woman who was all about growth and development. During our introduction, she gave us a blessing to go and experiment, and fail. To try our wings, to see what we could do, and learn from it. I could feel the enthusiasm within me. I could feel the engagement of really wanting to be connected and testing my abilities in that place.

Then, after she finished, the Chairman of the Department of Chaplaincy stood up and gave his talk. My supervisor's talk was about growth and challenging ourselves. The Chair of the department gave his talk about being careful and not causing embarrassment for the department. My enthusiasm was quickly dashed. One gave me a message of growth; the other gave me a message of carefulness. While not entirely incompatible, these two perspectives are certainly polarized.

I remembered, even then, consciously noting the two messages that were being given to all of us. I have come to realize that these two pieces reside in each of us. Each is a voice that we have taken in from our past. The voices fight each other in our heads. My supervisor's voice was a call to show up. The Chair of the department's voice was the call to be smaller, constricted, to not show up. I don't think that's what he meant. But his own fears and his own concerns blocked him from giving us a message of growth. Throughout that semester, I wrestled with those two messages. I found it hard to follow both messages at the same time. So I did not always show up as a chaplain. Sadly, I constricted my own growth, and ironically, that meant that I was of less service and help for the people under my care. I could have been a better chaplain had I shown up more often.

The problem was not with the Chair of the department, but with the fact that I allowed his message to be an internalized voice within me. I allowed that to activate a lesson — the pain and scars from the past. And when I did that, I constricted.

Playing small does not serve you, and it does not serve your relationships or marriage. It does not serve the world.

We live in a world where too many people don't show up. We live in a world where we choose to play small, plan carefully, and play within the constrictions. What potential opportunities do we miss in that process?

Remember, as humans, we are built for connection. Our brain is wired for connection with other humans. This deep connection is part of the reason that we take in those lessons of life to limit us. Lessons are learned in the midst of connection. In fact, if I have no connection with someone, I rarely internalize the message from that person.

You may ask, if we're wired for connection, then why are relationships so difficult?

Our desire for connection is mirrored by our fear of losing connection. Due to the fact that I desire connections so intensely, I'm fearful of losing them, of being disconnected.

So, to hedge my bets, I stay a bit distant. "What if I really connected with someone, and then I was rejected?" That's the fear that lurks in our heads. If I fully engage with someone, I'll leave myself open to the possibility of rejection, of losing that connection. So, we don't love with abandon, but with caution.

Two people love each other and decide to get married. At that point in their relationship, they can't imagine anything but wanting to be with the other person. Their growing relationship has fired up their connection. The connection has grown stronger and stronger. So, they decide to get married. But over time, on an unconscious level, each realizes the fear of losing that connection. So, each backs off a bit and both play it safe. But, each doesn't want the other person being distant. We all want full engagement from the other person, even if we're playing a little bit safe, ourselves. The problem is, when one person plays it safe, it feeds the fear of disconnection in the other person, which leads the other person to play it safe, which leads to both playing safer, which leads them both to play it safer. And so the pattern plays out. Our human desire for connection is matched by the fear of loss of connection.

Over time, the feelings of love and connection might wane, unless one or the other decides to really show up.

So What Would Showing Up Look Like With A Spouse?

All of us are scriptwriters in our head. We all deserve an Academy award for the scripts we write. In fact, in any conversation between two people there are three conversations going on most of the time.

There's the conversation that's going on with the other person, and the one that is going on inside of each person's head. We "write" the dialogue in our mind that we think should be spoken; at the same time the other person is writing the dialogue he or she thinks should be spoken. Here's the problem: the dialogues don't match up, which means we are constantly in the process of rewriting the script.

During a conversation, most of the time, people are thinking about the next thing they need to say, rather than listening to what is being said by the other person. That fuels the disconnection. That keeps us from showing up. If I'm waiting for the next opportunity for me to say my lines that I think should be spoken, and the other person is doing the same thing, neither one of us is truly showing up. We're having the conversation in our heads and not really between two people.

So to show up with a spouse is to be truly engaged in what's being said.

In my work as a therapist, working with couples, I am keenly aware of how often the question in the room was who is right and who is wrong. So, the couple has a conversation that is based on rightness and wrongness, not in connection and listening. So instead, they argue. My definition of an argument is two different people with two different opinions trying to convince each other of the rightness of his or her particular view. A conversation is an exchange of ideas. An argument is waiting for your chance to deliver the next part of your argument.

Arguments are entirely unhelpful and counterproductive. Intense conversations are not the problem; arguments are the problem. An intense conversation can be two people each trying to understand where the other person is coming from. An argument is each person trying to deliver his or her winning oration. I realized that in my counseling office, couples were trying to get me to be the arbiter of their issues. Arguments are won in the courtroom; they are not won in relationships. Instead, arguments tend to tear down a relationship. They tend to constrict the relationship. They stop the flow of connection between a couple.

In Don't Sweat The Small Stuff, Richard Carlson says "You can either be right or you can be happy, but you can't be both." An argument is an attempt to establish "rightness." A conversation is an invitation to understanding — and happiness.

What's The Alternative?

What if, instead, each person is listening for understanding, each person risks just listening in order to understand where the other person is coming from? We often get caught up in wanting to make our point, versus understanding someone else's point.

Let me clarify an important point. There is a substantial difference between understanding where somebody is coming from and agreeing with what that person is saying. I believe that our deep need as human beings is to be understood, not to have everybody agree with us. In a marriage, our need is to feel understood by our spouse, not to have our spouse necessarily agree with us.

So showing up is about listening for understanding in the conversation. One of my suggestions for couples in the middle of a conversation, before it turns to the well-trodden path of an argument, is to ask the simple question: "Can you help me understand how you see it that way?" For couples who have habituated to arguing, it's important to notice the delivery of those words is not meant to be made sarcastically, in a way that expresses that whatever the other person says has nothing to do with reality. Instead, it's delivered in a tone-neutral way. Think about a tone that I might use to say, "The sky is blue," or more accurately, "Isn't the sky blue?"

Because our hurt leads to anger, couples who have established a pattern of arguing will find it a challenge to change their communication pattern immediately. It will take a little effort to change the habit of interaction. We often fall into the trap of asking a question and then not really listening to the response. Instead, we are just waiting for our chance to express our own opinion. But stopping for a moment and really paying attention to a spouse's response is Showing Up.

How do ***you*** show up with your spouse? What if you take on the challenge for yourself, of staying away from the hurt and the resultant anger, and seeking to understand. What might happen then? What's possible in a relationship, if you change *your* side, in an attempt to show up by seeking understanding, not to have the other person understand you, but for you to understand the other person?

Showing Up is independent of the actions of the other person. You can always choose to show up, regardless of whether the other person follows suit. In fact, if you wait for your spouse to show up, you have doomed the process and potentially the relationship. Your responsibility is to decide to show up, on your own, regardless of what the other person does.

So the next time you have a conversation, and you realize it's moving toward an argument, speak to understand. Ask the question, "Can you help me understand how you see it that way?"

Showing Up In Daily Life

When is the last time you asked your spouse how his or her day was and really listened to the answer? How do you show up with your spouse on a daily basis? You listen to him or her about the day. You pay attention to what's going on in life.

When I say "pay attention," I'm not talking about the recitation of your spouse's daily schedule, but the emotions behind it. "Showing up" is about being engaged in each other's emotional life.

Conversations happen on two levels. The first level is **content**. Content is the stuff of what happened. It is the "facts of the day," what you did, what you said, what was said to you, etc. This is the superficial level. That does not mean it is unimportant, but only that it is a recitation of the facts. It stays on the surface, based in action and incident.

The second level is **process**. Process is the level of emotions and feelings. It is not just what happened, but how someone feels about what happened. It is about how someone creates meaning about the daily events of life.

We don't connect over content. We connect over process.

What often happens, though, is that couples get trapped in the world of content. They talk about their day — at least the schedule of their day, the life of their kids, and facts about money, household chores, and other life events.

Left out of that conversation is a conversation about the process — the feelings and emotions of each other. People connect in the midst of attending to and talking about process. ***We show up when we are attending to process, emotions, and meaning.***

Again, it's not that content is unimportant; it is important for couples to know what's going on in each other's lives. But in terms of connection and showing up, it's more important to know what's going on inside of the other person — a spouse's inner life. At this level, the question is: how is your spouse dealing with the content of your spouse's life?

So how do we get to the process level of a discussion? We ask. That is a good starting point. But asking requires awareness. *Awareness is part of the Showing Up.*

Awareness begins with an understanding that there is even a level of communication below content. While we all understand that to some degree, we don't often think about this level. So, having an awareness of this level is reconnecting with that level.

Notice the emotions behind the words. When your spouse is talking about an event, listen for the tone and emotions that might be behind it. Work to respond to the emotions behind the words. For instance, if your spouse is talking about the busy day, you may see some weariness in the words and note, "Wow, that sounds like a busy day! You must be exhausted. Was it frustrating?"

Attending to the *process* level of communication also keeps you out of the "fix it" mode that many spouses slip into. Attending to the emotions and feelings, the meaning behind the events, keeps you from needing to give advice or to try to fix the situation. It is simply a matter of listening to what is behind the words and supporting the emotions that are connected with the events.

Showing Up happens when you are responding to the process. When you only respond to the content, there will be little feeling of connection. It is only a recitation of the schedule — not particularly satisfying to either party.

Relationships Aren't Ever On Hold

When I work with couples with troubled marriages, a central theme often emerges. The theme is that one or the other person thought that the relationship was "on hold". They thought that they would raise the kids, get the career started, build up their life savings, and then get on with their marriage. But relationships aren't like that. Relationships are only growing or contracting.

There is no pause button for a relationship. Couples who place themselves on "pause" will only become disconnected over time. Relationships that are nurtured will grow. And relationships that are ignored will contract.

It's like growing a plant. You can't place a plant in suspended animation. You're either feeding and watering the plant, and watching it grow. Or, you are letting it die from lack of food, attention, and water.

I can't claim I have much of a green thumb, but I do like plants. After we moved into our new house, I did some landscaping in the front. The previous owners clearly had little concern for the outside of the house. They kept it up, but designed everything for low maintenance. There was not a lot of greenery and growth around. So, my wife and I decided to change that. I dug up the old dying stuff, we dug out the rocks that they had used around the house, and we planted new plants. And here's where the trouble started. Again, I don't claim a green thumb. I planted the plants, watered them some, but was not as intentional as I should have been. Many of the plants survived on their own, thanks to the soil and the fact that it did rain periodically. But there were a few that needed a little more attention — attention they didn't get.

I intended to water the plants but put it off to another day. I didn't see how it would make much of a difference if I watered today or tomorrow, and so I would put it off. The next day, I often put it off again. One day, to my surprise, the brown spots on the inside of the plants spread to the outside. It wasn't as noticeable at first, and I just thought the brown spots were some areas that had died off. But as it spread, I realized that the plants were dying from lack of water.

I immediately became more intentional. I watered more regularly. I paid more attention to them. I tried to trim out the dead spots. Some of the plants, I was able to save. But many, by the time I had noticed the brown, were irretrievable. I had to cut them down, dig them out, and replant.

It's the same with relationships. We often put off to another day what's most important because other things seem urgent. The rush of everyday life is rarely about showing up. Showing up is attending to the important things: The connection. The love. Spending time together.

Unfortunately, relationships can look healthy on the outside long after they have withered on the inside. The "brown" hasn't made it to the edges yet, and so we miss the signs at the early stages. Suddenly, one day, we're surprised to discover that a relationship is in trouble.

Over and over, I hear from couples who tell me that from the outside, everybody thinks they have the perfect marriage. But inside, they're completely disconnected. In those relationships, the couple failed to show up with each other and to the relationship.

One part of showing up in a relationship is spending time

together. But time isn't enough. Time is just the starting point. If you're not spending time together, there's no way to show up. But just because you spend time together does not mean that you are showing up for the other person.

I often send couples on dates. But I give them these rules: first, they cannot talk about the children, and second, they cannot talk about work. When I mention the idea of a date, both people are generally receptive to the idea. In fact, they're usually excited about the fact that they are going to be intentional about spending time together. They think it's a great idea and look forward to the time together. Until I tell them the rules. Then, the expressions often change.

After a glazed moment of reflection, I often get the same question, "Then what will we talk about?"

I then ask the couple to think about the conversations they had when they fell in love. Were they talking about the kids? Were they talking about work? Or were they talking about things that were deeper and more important than daily work life? Usually, without realizing it, we fall in love over conversations of internal process. We talk about our dreams, our beliefs, our expectations, and our hopes. We reveal ourselves: the parts that we revealed before fear got in our way; the parts that we shared before the scars and pains constricted us and kept us from sharing our true selves. So that's what I suggest couples talk about.

A marriage on hold is headed for trouble, starved and thirsting for connection. But this is a simple issue to remedy when you choose to show up and attend to the connection.

Showing Up To Hopes And Dreams

We all have dreams, hopes, and aspirations. We just stop sharing them. They don't go away.

But people get out of the habit of talking about deeper things, choosing instead to talk about content. You have to show up to have a conversation about process. There is nothing worse than sharing your hopes, dreams, and aspirations with someone who's not really listening and is not really present.

Can you imagine telling someone the deepest, most important things in your life, only to be met with "That's nice." Or worse yet, met with resistance and negativity. Henry David Thoreau said

"Friends. . . They cherish one another's hopes. They are kind to one another's dreams." Families are even more so. And for spouses, that support of dreams and hopes is critical.

Showing up is about supporting another person's dreams and hopes. They may not work out, but time will tell that. Many strange and wonderful things happen when hopes and dreams are given room to expand and grow. You don't know what's coming your way or how things will come together. When people really believe in their own dreams, hopes, and aspirations, they may go to great lengths to make them happen. And, the people who love them, who are calming when the fears of life swirl, will help them move in that direction.

We show up when we help people in creating, developing, and expanding their dreams and their hopes. We show up when we listen to their dreams, their hope, and their aspirations. We show up when we are fully invested and committed to hearing about what's important to the other person.

If you are out of practice, showing up with your spouse will take some effort. You both may be used to having important things ignored, or you may be used to protecting the important things, not revealing them to even your spouse. That's about fear. We stop sharing out of fear. Our deepest dreams are tender places for all of us. We often prefer to not share them just because we are afraid they won't be accepted, that the dreams will be seen as foolish, or that somehow they will be discounted. So we play it small with our dreams and our hopes.

Showing up with your spouse is about listening to their dreams and their hopes. It's about listening to their process, their internal emotional world. But it is also about risking sharing your own dreams, hopes, and aspirations. It's about you being engaged in the process of sharing your important parts with your spouse. Will a spouse always treat those dreams and hopes as the tender pieces of you that they are? No.

Remember, your spouse has his or her own scars pain and constriction. Sometimes, there are limits on the potential of what your spouse can be for you. Those limits come from hurts and pains in the past. It's not about you. It's about your spouse's own constriction.

Remember, your spouse is also doing the best your spouse can, given where your spouse is. This core belief is crucial. It allows you to continue to show up, even when you might feel your spouse is not showing up.

Showing Up To Your Own Hopes And Dreams

What about you? I just discussed showing up in listening to your spouse, paying attention to the process behind the content, and supporting your spouse's hopes and dreams.

But to really show up, you need to be in touch with your own hopes and dreams. You need to be showing up in your own life. When you are not in touch with that part of your life, you will be cut off from your own source of energy.

Moving through life, sliding from one event to another, but not connected to your own internal world, will leave you hollow and empty. As you continue to put energy out into the world, you will find that you are disconnected from your own source of energy. In your disconnection, you will play smaller and smaller. You may tell yourself (and others) that you are "burned out." But the real issue is you are unplugged. "Burning out" implies that you have spent all of yourself. Being unplugged means that you are not engaged because you are disconnected.

Let's talk about the practical side of reconnecting (plugging in) to your life. First, when someone is plugged in, they become much more attractive. This attraction is to yourself — you will want to get up, want to embrace the day, and want to discover/learn/explore the world. This attraction is to your spouse — your spouse will find you much more interesting and magnetic when you are plugged in. This attraction is to the world — more opportunities and possibilities emerge when people are truly plugged in.

So before I go on, are you plugged in? Have you connected with your own energy source? If so, you can skip on to the next session. If not, let's work on getting plugged in.

Plugging In and Showing Up In Three Steps

I truly believe we are designed to be plugged in, to show up in our own lives. When we are not, we simply need to discover how to get out of our own way.

Imagine yourself, your connection to that energy source, much like a cork. When you hold that cork down, it appears that it isn't floating. But if you just let go, it bobs immediately to the surface.

So how are you holding that cork down?

Many people discover the real issue is simply a misunderstanding of thoughts. So let me point out the obvious: thoughts are just thoughts. A thought going through your mind is simply that — a thought. It is not real, does not mean anything, and may represent no reality.

The problem is not the thought. That is just what a mind does: it creates thoughts. The problem is that we tend to forget that it is a thought. We confuse it with reality. We forget we are thinking and believe the thought is real.

Let me clarify: I am not discussing metaphysics. I am not examining how we might be creating a reality, bringing a world around us into being. I am speaking from a practical perspective.

Perhaps an example will clarify further. Let's assume that I am standing behind a desk. A metaphysical discussion may center around the amount of "empty space" that is in the desk, or perhaps a metaphysical discussion would center on how I created a reality of that table.

But for this example, let's just assume that the table is standing there. I may have a thought, "Why did someone put this table in front of me, blocking my way? How inconsiderate!" If I follow this thought, "entertaining" this thought, I could quickly become frustrated and angry at whomever might have willfully blocked my path.

It is also possible, though, to have the thought, "How considerate someone was to place this table here, so that I can place this heavy box on it!" Notice that both are simply thoughts. One might leave me in a bad mood, and the other might leave me in a good mood. But both are simply thoughts. Neither is more real at this point than the other. Both may be false, and either may be true.

My point is that the thought, not the actual event, has an emotional impact upon me. One thought leaves me feeling negative, and the other leaves me feeling positive. When we forget we are thinking, our emotional health is impacted because we end up buying into the thoughts.

So Step #1 to plugging in and showing up is: understanding that *A Thought Is Just A Thought.*

This step does not require **not** thinking. That is, in my opinion, impossible. A mind is designed to create thoughts. It is what a mind does, and it cannot be stopped. It is, instead, **thought realization**. This is an awareness that the thought you are having is just a thought. And this realization helps to pull one away from the emotional impact of a thought.

Let's assume that you might be having some thoughts about how much your spouse does not love you, does not want you around, and therefore how impossible it is to save your marriage. Even if your spouse has told you this, being aware that this is a thought helps you to find a little distance from your own thought. It ***may*** be true, but the fact is that this is just a thought. But instead of allowing the thought to come and go (the design of our mind), we tend to grab onto the thought and just continue to be stuck on it, growing the thought along the way. We pull in more and more fear, think about it more and more, and find ourselves trapped deeper and deeper under the thought.

My strategy, when I find myself wrapped up in my thought, is to say "That's just a thought. I can let it go." Strangely, the thought begins to evaporate as soon as I note it is just a thought. It might come back. But I then repeat the same thing again, "That's just a thought. I can let it go."

Remember, *A Thought Is Just A Thought.*

This brings us to the next step. This step is to help plug you into your own energy source — those ideas, activities and dreams that bring you energy. Are you the typical person that is so busy putting out fires and dealing with the life that is right in front of you that you neglect those areas that energize you?

Let's think about this in two ways.

Exercise #1: Your Active Life

1) List the activities and interests that make you feel alive. Write down the hobbies and interests in which you have participated in the past.

2) Place a checkmark beside those activities in which you *regularly* participate. You must define *regularly,* but I often have people who come up to me and announce, "I'm a SCUBA diver, too!" I respond, "Great! Where'd you dive last?" Nine times out of ten, I am met with, "Oh, I went diving ten years ago, when I got certified." That is

not *regularly* diving, for instance! So use your own sense of regular participation and be honest. This list is only for you.

3) Beside each item in which you do not regularly participate, write the reasons why you do not regularly participate.

4) Examine each reason. Is it a reason or an excuse?

5) Choose how you might involve yourself in the activities and interests that you have already noted make you feel alive.

So Step #2, Involve Yourself In Activities and Interests That Make You Feel Alive.

Exercise #2: Your Life List

I love the idea of a list of things you want to experience in your lifetime. I call it a Life List. Others call it a Bucket List. I just don't like the idea that you are trying to get it end before you die. Instead, it is a list that will enhance your life.

1) Spend a few days writing down (yes, actually writing them down) a list of all the experiences you want to have in your lifetime. Make them specific and clear.

2) Do not censure this list based on practicality or expense. Your method of making sure something stays on the list is simply whether or not you get excited by it. If you write it down and you don't get excited when you look at it, that item is likely somebody else's dream — not yours.

3) Do not include achievements you want to have at work or in terms of income. Make sure it is in your control. For example, "I want to write a book" is great (and fully in your control). But "I want to write a bestseller" is problematic (because it is not in your control). Similarly, "I want to earn $1 million" probably should not be on this list. It may be a great financial goal, but not an experience for plugging into life.

4) Choose 1 to 3 of these items and begin thinking about how you can make them happen.

5) Check off the "Done" items as you complete them.

6) Repeat as long as possible.

So Step #3, Seek Out Experiences That Make You Feel Alive.

If you are doing these items and you are not plugged into your energy source, you have likely not been honest with your assessment of activities and experiences that bring you life and/or you are still buying into your thoughts!

When you are plugged in, it will be easier and easier to **Show Up**.

CHAPTER 10
C-REATE A NEW PATH

As you work to reconnect and you work to change yourself, the next step is charting a new course, *Create a New Path*. This is a critical step. Do not underestimate it or ignore it. You are attempting to get your spouse to join you on a journey. Just like any journey, your fellow traveler is going to want to know where you are headed. Otherwise, why join the process? Likewise, until you know *where* you are going, why would you start the journey?

Simply being connected and changing your self is not enough. These are activities that prepare you for an entirely new relationship. And while they need to be continual efforts, they only create the foundation for what you want: a deeply engaged and enriching relationship with your spouse that takes you through the journey of life — that provides you with a relationship you both treasure, companions through the good times and rough times.

The first two steps are about preparing for this journey. The connection provides the basis of why each of you will travel together. Your efforts to change yourself have started a process that prepares you to face the future with a new strength and vitality. Creating a new path is about mapping the journey — and then following your map!

A beginning question is this: do you know where you are headed? Many people *think* they know the path, but then find the path they were following was full of dead-ends and false starts. This should really be no surprise. Marriage is a misunderstood relationship. More than that, marriage has an intensity that pulls people off the path, unless they are sure of their way.

Have you ever been walking a trail in the woods? I'm not talking about a clearly marked trail, but one that is faint and somewhat indistinct? Imagine that you decide to go for a hike. Some people point you to a "trailhead," a clear point at the edge of a parking lot that goes into the woods. They point you toward that opening in the trees, pat you on the back, and wish you well on your hike.

So, a bit ill-prepared, under-dressed, and carrying way too little food and water, you charge off into the woods. The trail is fairly distinct and clear for several hundred yards. You can still hear the families in the parking lot, so you feel pretty secure. "How hard could the trail be?," you ask yourself

But as you go a bit further, the trail gets a bit more difficult to see. Sometimes, you can't be sure if the cut through the bush is really a trail. It could just be a dry spot. Or maybe just a cut-through the animals have created. But you keep on charging forward. At several points, you see where it appears the trail might cut off to one side or the other. You pause to consider, but still decide to push on.

With every fork in the trail, every time you have to choose a direction, you begin to doubt your capacity of navigating the woods. You realize that when people told you, "Don't worry. This is an easy trail. Just get started. You will see where to goes," they provided no useful information. They gave you confidence. But now, you are wondering if it is false confidence, as you are wandering through ever darker and thicker woods.

After awhile, you are not even sure if you can find your way back. As you look behind you, the forest seems to close around you. It's getting a bit cold, your water and food are low, and you are not sure how far it might be ahead. They never told you how far it was, nor how serious your situation could get. And here you are, the sun setting, lost in the woods.

A little scary, right? These are just the right ingredients to activate those fears. Even if you feel fairly confident that you can see the path, you start doubting yourself. What if you took the wrong trail? What if there isn't any trail, after all. What if the path just keeps getting worse? Even if you are on the right path, the doubts can creep in and cause you to make costly errors. Fear does that.

Now compare that with arriving at the trailhead. Some people told you it can get cool out there, so you have the proper clothes. A rain jacket is in your backpack, just in case of a storm. "Better safe than sorry," they told you. There is plenty of water and food.

But more than that, the trail is well marked. And even better, the people told you what the trail would look like. They told you about some landmarks. As you pass the landmarks, you have renewed confidence that you are on the right trail, headed in the right direction. You continue to look for the trail markers described to you. If they had not warned you, you might have missed them. Instead, you see them and know you are headed in the right direction.

Even the descriptions about the rougher parts of the trail help you to get past them. They told you that some places are rocky and a bit tough to get across, but then the path gets better, and the vista rewards your efforts, so you keep moving forward.

Every now and then, you doubt yourself, and your fear creeps in. But then, you see a mark or simply remind yourself that your path is clear and you know where you are headed. So, the fear evaporates. You make good choices, based on confidence — and you enjoy the entire hike, even the challenges!

Option #1: Wander down an unknown path. Try to invite someone along to join you on that trip!

Option #2: Take a journey down a path, leading to a clear destination. Is it easier to get someone to join you when you know the way?

That's pretty much the story of marriage, isn't it? People point you toward the starting point and send you on your way, ill-prepared and unclear on where to go, which is why we see so many marriages in trouble. How can you get somewhere, if you didn't know where you are trying to get to?

Alice came to a fork in the road. "Which road do I take?" she asked.
"Where do you want to go?" responded the Cheshire Cat.
"I don't know," Alice answered.
"Then," said the Cat, "it doesn't matter."

—Lewis Carroll, *Alice in Wonderland*

A Crash-Course In Marriage

Sometimes, we really complicate things. Marriage is one of those things. But the process two people coming together and forming a life together has been happening for a very long time — much longer than self-help books and experts have been around. In fact, the "experts" seem to have done little to help make marriages work.

Perhaps our theories really only serve to complicate. That is the nature of humans. We really like to complicate things. Remember my years as a magician? The best tricks were always the simplest. But what really entertained me was the way people would come up with very complicated methods they thought I was using to do the trick. One small trick took one simple sleight-of-hand move to work. But people would expound with long explanations on the mechanics of the "wand" I used for the trick. They took so long looking for a mechanical explanation worthy of a master engineer, that they missed one simple movement I made.

The same is true with many explanations of living. The more complicated we make it, the more lost we become. The more overwhelmed we become, the less confident we become.

So for just a moment, let us assume together that marriage is really pretty simple. The goal of marriage is only this: to become a WE.

With that, I could end your crash-course. That is all you really need to know. Create a WE and you are done. You will have a life-long learning task of building that sense of WE, but you have the answer. Sure, there are unconscious/subconscious/conscious levels to this. That is true with everything we do. Marriage is no different.

But if two people are working to build a WE, they are going to be unstoppable!

If only people knew that was the task, from even before they got married — but at least by the time they marry. If they knew that, then the path becomes much clearer. The task becomes much simpler. (Remember that "simple" is not the same as "easy.")

So let's talk a bit about what it means to be a WE, and some ways to build/rebuild that, even if you have found yourself lost in the woods. You may discover that you are either on the path, or just off to the side.

Let me suggest some rules for building this new path.

Creating A New Path

Now it is time to create a new path. That path is probably new for you, so I want to make sure you have very clear guidelines on how to blaze this trail. Remember that this path is forged together, but also remember that one person can start the process. But also remember that "starting the process" is NOT telling your spouse what he or she needs to be doing. This is not an insistence that he or she start down the path ahead of you.

Since you are the one ready to see a change in the relationship, you will be leading the process of creating a new path. And you may find that your spouse is not excited about heading down this path. Remember, all your spouse can see is a dark woods with a poorly marked trailhead that disappears into the woods. Your spouse is going to be unclear on whether this trail is good. And your spouse is probably also unsure as to whether he or she even wants to go down another trail together. You will need to hold a vision of your destination in your head.

Let's jump in and look at some of the rules (or guidelines) for creating this new path, so that you have your navigational skills ready to go.

9 Rules To Creating A New Path

1) Marriage is misunderstood. This is why you both have missed the mark so far. It isn't your fault that you haven't gotten there. If you don't know the goal, it is very hard to get there!

This is important to remember for yourself and for your spouse.

First, realize it for yourself, so that you can be open to something new. And more than that, you can stop blaming yourself for the fact that you are having difficulties. So take it in: if you don't know what you are trying to achieve, you can't blame yourself that you did not get there.

Then take in the next step in development: once you know where to go, you CAN take responsibility to get there. And remember the difference between ***blame*** ("Who is at fault here?") and ***responsibility*** ("What can *I* do to change where we are?")

Second, realize it for your spouse. Just as you are blameless for not getting there, so is your spouse. Not only this, but if you didn't know where you are going, the intimacy of a marital relationship will strain a relationship (when it is off-course) and cause both of you to act in less-than-optimal ways (a nice way to say that it is likely neither of you have been particularly loving or nice toward each other lately). Knowing this, can you take a risk and let go of the pain? Can you seek to be forgiving of your spouse? Can you let him/her "off the hook" for not getting any closer to the goal than you?

Remember, people do the best they can, where they are. When we find a better way to be, most people do it — at least when they are willing to let go of the hurt and move forward.

2) The new path is about being a *WE (but there are some fears that will arise).* We have established that getting to *WE* is what we are headed toward. **WE** is the relationship you want to create — and it requires two pieces: connection and self-growth. The first two C's of this process are what create the capacity of building a WE. Part of being a WE is based on feeling a strong connection with your spouse. Part of being a WE is being a strong "me." You have to bring your best self into the relationship. Otherwise, the fears of intimacy will derail you.

We all have two central fears around a close relationship:

1) The fear of intimacy.

2) The fear of abandonment.

The fear of intimacy is a fear we all have. This is the fear that, if we get too close, we will lose ourselves to the other person. It is the fear that you will have to give up your self — your opinions, desires, hopes, and dreams. This fear of intimacy creates a distancing from the relationship. When the fear of intimacy is activated, people create distance, pick fights, argue over unimportant issues, and take opposing opinions just to oppose.

The fear of abandonment is a fear we all have. This is the fear that the person with whom we feel a strong connection will abandon us, leaving us "out in the cold." When captured by a fear of abandonment, many people will either: a) abandon first or b) cling tightly — too tightly. We will either "beat the other person to the punch" and "run out the door" before the other person can do it to us, or we will try to prevent the person from leaving by holding on to them, becoming too desperate and needy.

We ALL have both of these internal fears. We ALL can be triggered to fear either intimacy or abandonment, which is why intimate relationships — marriage being the most intimate, can be difficult to navigate, if you do not understand this dynamic.

Imagine the complication that can happen when two people are experiencing these fears at the same time! Here is where it gets more complicated with two: what a person does to combat one fear will likely trigger the opposite fear in the other person.

For example, if I fear intimacy, I will withdraw emotionally; then, I might trigger a fear of abandonment in my spouse. When that happens, my spouse might try to move a bit closer, cling a little tighter. When that happens, it deepens my fear of intimacy. So I withdraw more — deepening my spouse's fears, who then tries to pull closer. Around and around we might go, both gripped by the opposite fear and deepening the fear in each other.

At some point, given enough fear, the relationship will collapse, unable to sustain the fear levels in each person.

But what happens if we were to live *into* a connection, a sense of being in it together, no matter what?

A commitment to stay together, no matter what, can transform the relationship. Stepping into a deep commitment allows each to feel the commitment of two individuals to be something bigger than either as individuals — without risk of abandonment or risk of losing the self.

Being a *WE* is not about a "mind meld" where each person disappears into the conglomerate. It is about two individuals choosing to come together to love and support each other, bringing their skills and gifts into the relationship, to get through life together. That requires each person to step into the relationship, bringing their best to the equation and recognizing that there is no threat of the relationship ending.

True intimacy is not about becoming "carbon copies" of each other; it is about treasuring the differences and honoring the commitment of two different people to make it through life, each protecting the relationship and treasuring the other person.

(If you want more information on my model of intimacy, please see my Save The Marriage System.)

3) Being A WE starts from within yourself. It is important to recognize this: start with YOU! Do not look at your spouse and demand that he or she join you in being a *WE*. When a marriage is in trouble, your spouse will be unwilling to jump in. So don't demand that.

Start the process within yourself.
Don't wait for your spouse.
Start with yourself.

**This is important: a large part of being a *WE* (much more than a majority) happens in your mind. While it is optimal for this to be happening in BOTH of your minds, you can start the process with it happening in YOUR mind.

Millennia ago, couples existed. At that time, they did not have the time to "talk about their feelings," did not worry about "quality time together," did not go to seminars or retreats or workshops, and certainly not therapists. They worked hard to protect the family. They stood together and worked to make it through life together — a much more substantial challenge than it is today.

The difference? They knew their survival depended on staying together as a unit. They carried with them the sense that they were in it together. It was not something that would have been discussed; it was simply something that each acted upon.

That is a choice that you, too, can make. You can choose to adopt an approach of being a WE, even if your spouse is not acting in that way. Here is an important point: ***when one person adopts this stance, often, the other person will follow.***

Being a *WE* touches that deepest need for connection that we humans have. It becomes attractive on a deep and unconscious level, even if your spouse first pushes against it.

As you assume a stance of being a WE, the path becomes attractive to the other spouse. It is magnetizing because of the deep desire we have to join with another person — it is programmed into our genes and our minds.

(NOTE: There are times when relationships have deteriorated so far that a spouse resists all efforts to build a WE. The spouse may have already formed a connection with another person or may simply be at a point of such deep hurt and disdain that he or she is simply unwilling to move in this direction. That said, I

am often amazed at the capacity for moving in this direction to heal the deep hurts and bring a couple back together. I am sometimes surprised on both how long or how short it takes to gain traction. Keep working at this, even if you begin to lose hope. Maintain that image of your ideal life/relationship that you constructed at the beginning. When you feel frustrated and hopeless, read back through what you wrote.)

You can start the process of becoming a WE right now. Begin by looking at life by what is best for the WE — you *and* your spouse. Whenever there is a decision to be made, consider this question: "What is best for US? What is best for the WE?"

This question gets you past "You/Me Thinking." In You/Me Thinking, there is a winner and a loser. Someone gets what they want, and the other person loses out. Even if you make a decision that favors your spouse (and therefore are patting yourself on the back for not looking after yourself), you are still stuck in "you/me," which leads to resentment and a power struggle. Either you or your spouse will struggle (or both) when the decision is made as you/me.

Whenever there is a power struggle, you can be sure that you are NOT in *WE*.

Let me warn you: if you are out of practice, thinking in terms of "What is best for us?" will be a struggle. It will be a challenge to think creatively, but the solution is usually much better than the simple "you or me" solutions.

4) Don't expect your spouse to be at the same place. In other words, don't expect (and certainly don't demand) your spouse to be thinking about *WE* or acting as a *WE*.

Your spouse is likely hurt at this point. Hurt expresses itself as anger. Anger is repelling. And that repelling nature is anathema to being a WE.

Let's make an assumption that you may be a little angry, too. And behind your anger is hurt. But there is a difference between where you are and where your spouse is — you have a little more information. You have a new puzzle piece that makes the struggle make sense. You understand something that your spouse does not.

Don't expect your spouse to be at that place. Expect that YOU will move to that place.

A marriage is very much like an algebraic equation. If you change one side of the equation, the other side will also make a change.

Change your side of the equation. This is different than the typical, which is that each side adjusts to the other side, and usually at a lower level of functioning.

One person begins to move away from the relationship. The other person responds by shifting away from the relationship. This equalizes the equation for just a moment, until one person makes another shift away from the relationship. This is matched by another shift away by the spouse. And as that process continues, the relationship begins to degrade toward zero, and then ends up in the negative numbers!

That is the unintentional and unconscious process. But the same process (though in the reverse direction) can happen when one person becomes conscious and intentional about that process. You are the one to start that process.

Make a commitment to move toward being a *WE*, even if you expect no movement from your spouse. In fact, let me request that you work very hard to NOT expect anything from your spouse. Simply commit to making the shift. You can, single-handedly, start the process of rebuilding, of shifting the equation toward the positive.

5) Create a VERY clear vision of what this looks like. I want you to look back on your statement of your ideal life and relationship. Read through it. It would surprise me if you do NOT find that statement representing being a *WE*. When most people express their ideal relationship, they describe being a WE, but don't realize it until they examine it through this lens of understanding. Once you have a new clarity to what the relationship should be, you can see this is what may have been unclearly defined before.

Go back to your statement of your ideal relationship. Now, rewrite it with a clearer understanding of what it means to be a *WE*.

Be as clear and specific as you can. Clarity is crucial. When you become clear, you will naturally move in that direction. Our brain is constantly looking for what we focus upon. Positive or negative, your brain's scanning system naturally moves toward whatever is activated in your mind. If you are focused on what you fear, you will move toward it. If you focus on what you want, and you are clear about it, you will move toward that. So your clear statement of being a *WE* is like uploading a new app into your operating system. The system will then begin moving in a new direction.

6) INVITE your spouse to join you. DON'T insist or preach. SHOW.

At some point in the process of saving your marriage, your spouse is going to have to join you. But the timing of that is with your spouse, not you. The choice to join the process must come from within your spouse. Pressure from outside will only lead to more resistance.

Motivational Psychology refers to this phenomenon as "*psychological reactance.*" Psychological reactance is the tendency for people to resist anything that seems to impinge on their freedom of choice. In other words, we tend to resist something that we feel is forced upon us, *even if we agree with it.* And that is the important point here. Even if your spouse agrees that there needs to be more connection, if your spouse feels forced into it, he or she will naturally resist.

And if your spouse is not entirely on-board with working on the marriage, the resistance will be even higher. This is often the case, that one spouse wants to improve the relationship and the other does not. Your spouse may either not see that there is that big of a problem or may have already moved toward giving up. In either case, trying to force your spouse to work on the relationship, in any way, will only lead to further resistance. It causes the spouse to either more loudly proclaim that nothing is wrong or more loudly proclaim that things are hopeless. There is no need to build an even higher fence for you to cross.

You want to invite your spouse into the process by your actions. This is not a formal invitation or a spoken request for your spouse to join the process of improving your relationship. It is more about becoming inviting in your actions. Much like making a room "more inviting," you want to have your actions create an inviting atmosphere for your spouse to *want* to be a part of the relationship.

Our tendency, as humans, is that once we gain some new level of understanding, we want everyone to see it our way. We want people to see "the truth." And we are generally convinced that we are seeing things more clearly than anyone else. That is just human nature — and not particularly useful in this context.

If you agree with me that marriage is about becoming a *WE*, then you have a new understanding. But be patient. Just because you have arrived at a new understanding does not mean that your spouse will be ready to jump in.

Simply be committed to acting as a WE. Make choices and decisions based on being a WE. Think of your relationship as a WE. Think of the two of you as a strong unit, standing as a single force, with the goal of getting through life together. Your mindset will show in your actions. Your spouse will see your actions. Your actions will invite your spouse into a new mindset.

7) Don't try too hard. Remember the playful approach, versus "working on it."

I have noticed that when there is a crisis, people become very serious. They put on their "work face" and dig in. Often, in the process, they strangle the life right out of whatever they are addressing. When people put on their "work face," they move away from their playful spirit. And when one steps away from that playful spirit, creativity evaporates.

Love and connection are, by nature, forged in playfulness and creativity. Think back to those days of dating and romance. Were they not playful? Were they not creative? That fact never changes, but how we approach the world does. We decide to "grow up" and be serious, which is often about the time that a relationship disconnects.

Do notice that there is a difference between being playful and being immature. This is not about "recapturing youth." We humans seem to have a hard time finding a healthy way of integrating a lighter approach to adulthood. It is as if we are either acting like children or being serious adults.

There is another layer, though. This is a layer of engagement. Engagement is all about *showing up*. You have already focused on this, so you are now ready to bring it into your marriage.

Let me give you just a brief example. One of my suggestions for people working to save a marriage is to not have those "relationship talks." You know the ones I am talking about? In your mind, you can have this wonderful discussion that clarifies the issue, gets you both on the same page, and gets you moving forward.

Almost every time, these talks fail. And almost every time, the talks end up having a spouse justify and rationalize even more about why the relationship is hopeless.

When we *talk* about a relationship, we stop *relating*. To have that discussion requires someone to climb up into their head, take on a persuasive approach, and disconnect from the heart and gut. Connection rarely comes from the logical/rational spot. When is the last time you said, "That person's logic was so perfect, I got hot for them!"? But when was the last time you said, "I really connected with that person! We were just on the same wavelength!" Connection does not come from talking about the relationship. It comes from relating. "Relating" requires you to show up.

Strike this phrase from your thinking: "We need to work on our marriage." Replace it with this phrase: "We can connect and relate."

Show up with your best self, work on the connection, and you begin to have a lighter approach to the process of transforming your marriage.

8) Power Struggles/Control will pull you off the path. In fact, whenever you find yourself in a power struggle or want to grab control, you will know that you are moving away from being a *WE*.

Confession time: after over 25 years of marriage, I still find those places where I lose track of the goal. I don't stop to think, "What's best for US?" And I usually discover that I have moved away from the relationship. Please understand that this does not mean I never do anything for ME. I exercise regularly, paddleboard, scuba dive, and spend time alone. So being a WE is not about being a "superglue couple," always bound together. It is a mental awareness that the goal of the marriage is to get through life together, taking care of each other and working toward building a connection that nurtures and nourishes all.

But there are times when that primitive part of my brain gets the better of me. I resort to power struggles. It doesn't end well for me, my wife, or our relationship. Then, we just have to re-gear and start again.

Some time ago, I remember my wife and I were having a "discussion." It was heated — and here is the irony, I have no idea what it was about anymore. As with most arguments, the content is irrelevant to the fact that the real issue is almost always simply a struggle for control or understanding.

Back to our little "discussion." Our argument had continued for a while, with neither of us really shifting our perspectives. (Do we ever in the midst of an argument?) During a lull, my wife went to the basement to do something. After she left, a rebuttal came to my mind that I just knew would turn the argument! Certainly, she would "see the light" and come to my perspective. Or so my primitive brain convinced me!

So, I followed her downstairs and started in on my point. My wife calmly turned to me and said, "Let me ask you a question. Is what you are about to say going to make any difference, if we are going to be together for the rest of our lives?" That stopped me in my tracks. There was *nothing* I had to say that mattered, because being together was not about winning an argument. The argument ended right there.

If you find yourself in the midst of a power struggle, you will know that you are not headed toward being a *WE*. As hard as it can be, disengage from the struggle and re-engage in the relationship.

9) Focus on *Connection + New Self = New Path.* That is your new equation. When you focus on connecting with your spouse and showing up with your best self, and you know that your new path is about being a WE, then you have the ingredients to save your marriage. But you need all the parts working together.

If you focus on connecting but are not becoming your best self, you will quickly become needy or manipulative. If you focus on being your best self but are not connecting, it will lead you away from the relationship. You will simply develop your individuality, but never move toward the relationship. If you focus on connecting and becoming your best self, but don't know your new path, you will feel closer and better, but will likely fall back into a disconnected power struggle down the road.

The equation only works when all three pieces are a part of the equation. When all are present, you have a clear path for rebuilding and transforming your marriage. It is an equation that will guide your marriage long after the relationship has been restored.

Notice that these are three simple steps: **Connect**, **Change** your self, **Create** a new path. But simple is not the same as easy. It requires you to step up and take action. It requires you to take responsibility, drop blame, and begin to connect, both with your higher self and with your spouse.

CHAPTER 11
WHAT NOW?

What a journey we have followed! When you arrived, you knew you wanted to save your marriage. Perhaps you had already tried several approaches. Or perhaps you were still gathering information, not quite sure where to start. Or perhaps you were still feeling very much lost. I hope you have now shifted to a new place of understanding and action.

At this point, you have a clear understanding of what it takes to both transform a marriage in trouble and keep that marriage on-track.

Remember that knowledge is only one element of the process. Knowledge without action — without *courageous* action, is worthless information. How are you applying this information? How have you been transformed? How have you been transforming the relationship?

The path to mastery is interesting, for any area. You have been on a path of mastery, both in relationship skills and in personal transformation. Sometimes, we lose track of our progress.

There are several points along that path of mastery:

1) You don't know what you don't know. This is a point of blissful (or painful) ignorance. You don't even know that there is a problem or that there is information you are lacking.

This is the beginning point for any journey. We all start here. That is the nature of life and the beginning point of learning. It is a place where many people remain. And if an area of life does not affect you, it is possible to stay frozen in not knowing what you don't know.

But when something is no longer working, when you reach the limits of the usefulness of the tools you have, something beckons you to make a shift. Sometimes, it is an opportunity or a curiosity. Often, it is a crisis. With relationships and personal growth, it is almost always a crisis that pulls us into the next stage.

2) You know what you don't know. At this point, you have become aware that there are some skills, tools, attitudes, or perspectives that are missing. As you begin to look around, you realize that there is so much more to discover.

If the reason is compelling enough, you take action to learn the new skills, discover new perspectives, and master a new area of life. If the reason is less compelling, you may simply lose interest, overwhelmed with a new body of information.

3) You know what you know. At this point, you are more aware of the skills you have discovered. You can point to the theories, strategies, and techniques you have learned and are implementing. When someone asks, "Why did you do that?" you can provide a theoretical explanation of the reason. At this point, you may still be mastering the application, but you understand the reasoning.

This is likely the point where you are right now. You may have some new techniques and understandings that are transforming you and your relationship. At times, you may be frustrated at the fact that you do not "do it perfectly." But you know what you are striving toward. Mastery of a new skill does not come overnight.

4) You don't know what you know. At this point, you have attained a level of skill that allows you to interact with the new approach on automatic. Your skill level means that you are acting and responding differently without much thought about it.

The difference between Level 3 and Level 4 is only one of practice. What at first feels awkward begins to feel more and more natural. A higher and higher percentage of the time, you respond in the "new" way (which is quickly becoming the "old" way, as it becomes the default). And, you see it working better and better.

Remember these points:

- ✓ We ALL start from a point of not knowing, of ignorance. It is the ONLY starting point there is.
- ✓ A change in attitude and/or behavior takes time, energy, effort, and courage. Doing anything differently is partly a matter of our brain creating a new neural network to replace the old method (our previously automatic response).
- ✓ It will always feel awkward at the beginning. Any new skill does. The only thing that makes it less awkward is to continue doing it.
- ✓ The in-between space — between the old way and the new way, can be frustrating, both for ourselves and those around us. That is a space where you take three steps forward and two steps back, as the old thought processes creep in. Be patient with yourself. Change is a challenge.
- ✓ The effort is worth it. The cost of staying where you were is heavy and rarely has a pay-off. The new perspective will offer more opportunity of possibility, even if it can feel a little scary.
- ✓ It is important to reinforce the change by noting the shifts you are making. You can also find other material that reinforces the changes you are making. Growth, once it starts, can continue with just a little effort. Seek out information that broadens your new perspective. But only seek out information as you are ready to implement. Information for information's sake will not lead to growth.

Creating A Plan

At this point, you have the information in front of you. If you are still reading, you know what you need to do (knowledge), you want to make a shift in your relationship (courage), and you have been making some changes (action).

In order to make sure you are staying on-track and do not get pulled back into old patterns of thinking and acting, it is a good idea to be intentional about creating your plan for saving and transforming your marriage.

There are three areas upon which you will want to focus:

Connecting With Your Spouse

- ✓ What methods, specifically, do you want to use in your effort to connect?
- ✓ What are the ways the two of you connected in the past?
- ✓ Think back to the ways you connected as you were falling in love. What actions made *your spouse* feel loved? (Don't get trapped into thinking about what your spouse did that made *you* feel loved.)
- ✓ How do you see your spouse showing appreciation and love to others? (This will give you some clues about how your spouse understands love.)
- ✓ Make a list of actions, attitudes, and perspectives to which you commit yourself in your attempts to reconnect.

Changing Yourself

- ✓ What are the areas in life where you have excused yourself and for which you need to take responsibility? (We all have them. We have to acknowledge them, in order to start the process of change.)
- ✓ What are the actions and attitudes that hold you back and are counter-productive to your personal growth? (These tend to be habits of action and thought that are limiting and even destructive.)
- ✓ What are the standards you have, that you need to raise to the next level? (Remember, a *standard* is what you expect of yourself.)
- ✓ Make a list of the actions, attitudes, and perspectives to which you commit yourself in your growth toward being your best self.

Creating A New Path

- ✓ Where are the places in your life in which you have not been acting as a *WE*?
- ✓ How, in the past, have you responded to fears of intimacy and/or fears of abandonment? How will you respond, intentionally, in a different way?
- ✓ How can you invest more in being a *WE*? (This is about you stepping into being a WE, not expecting your spouse to be

doing the same.)

- ✓ Make a list of the actions, attitudes, and perspectives to which you commit yourself in your efforts to create a new path for your relationship.
- ✓

Spend some time writing down your responses. This is not just a thought exercise. It is an exercise in intentionality, best done by writing it down and reviewing it frequently.

When we don't write down our plans, they tend to get lost in the busy shuffle of life. We lose track of what we intended to do. With the best of intentions, we end up reverting to old ways of responding.

More than that, saving your marriage is about existing in a world of emotions and turmoil. When the emotions get you, it is easy to forget the plan. It is easy to slide back into the place of hurt and reactivity. That place serves neither you nor your relationship. It is simply the primitive part of your brain that gets stuck in "fight/flight/freeze" behavior.

In those moments, remember a quote my wife often uses:

Consult your plan, not your feelings!

Feelings will lead us away from useful behavior when we are struggling. Your plan, though, is made in a moment of clear-headed thinking. It will keep you on-target and headed in helpful directions.

FINAL NOTE: GETTING MORE HELP FOR YOUR MARRIAGE

I hope that you have found the information in this book helpful. In fact, my hope is that the information is transformational, not just in your marriage, but in your life. I firmly believe that the steps outlined in this book contain the capacity of affecting all areas of your life. It is not just in marriage that people are haunted by limiting beliefs and fears.

But the starting point for your life transformation is your marriage. The three simple steps we have discussed in this book are truly the only three steps you must master in order to save and transform your marriage. You may, however, wish to have more information about exactly what to do, and exactly why you should do it.

For the past 10+ years, I have been helping couples around the world through my Save The Marriage System. This System provides you with step-by-step methods of addressing your situation, regardless of where it is.

In fact, the first place you will start in the System is an assessment of the stage of problem in your relationship. There are seven different stages, each one needing a separate approach.

The System will continue by helping you understand what your marriage can and should be. It addresses the specific issues of sex, money, and parenting. And included is a model to help you understand how to build intimacy and how to work through the "stuck" places around intimacy.

One of the major "stuck" places in many marriages is anger and resentment. We will focus some time and energy in understanding this dynamic and a method for dealing with these two corrosive emotions.

We will also tackle how to deal with a midlife marriage crisis and how to deal with infidelity in two very powerful audios. These audios will give you an understanding of why each crisis occurs and how to deal with it in constructive ways.

The best part? You get instant access to the System, no matter what time it is and where you are in the world.

Are you ready to take the next step in saving your marriage? If you are ready, grab my Save The Marriage System by going to **www.SaveTheMarriage.com**

ABOUT THE AUTHOR

Dr. Lee H. Baucom has been helping individuals and couples to save their marriage and improve their relationships for over 25 years. After his training as a marriage therapist, Dr. Baucom became disillusioned with the success record of marital therapy. After experimenting and testing, Dr. Baucom created his Save The Marriage System, a program that has helped thousands of couples around the world.

Dr. Baucom has been happily married for over 25 years, and has two children. He is proud of his family and wants others to have a similar experience in their own lives. When not working, Dr. Baucom enjoys trail running, paddle boarding, and scuba diving.

Printed in Great Britain
by Amazon